Cheryl J. Costley

Stitching to Dye
in Quilt Art

Colour, Texture and Distortion

Stitching to Dye
in Quilt Art

Colour, Texture and Distortion

C. June Barnes

BATSFORD

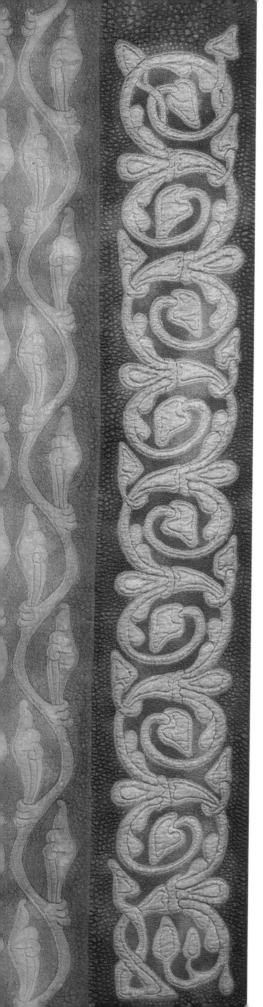

Acknowledgements

I dedicate this book to all those adventurous stitchers who have shared the journey. Long may you ask the question 'What if … ?'

I thank first and foremost a very tolerant Stuart who has always been there, uncomplaining and supportive; Leslie Morgan for showing me this door and helping (pushing) me through it; Penni Tarbuck for 'proofing' the exercises; Mum and Lee who help keep my body and soul together; all those who have lent pieces or provided photography of their wonderful work; Michael Wicks for his photography and my family and friends for being there when I needed them. Without you all I could not have done this!

First published in the United Kingdom in 2008 by
Batsford
10 Southcombe Street
London W14 0RA

An imprint of Anova Books Company Ltd

ISBN: 978 0 7134 9070 1

A CIP catalogue record for this book is available from the British Library.

16 15 14 13 12 10 09 08
10 9 8 7 6 5 4 3 2 1

Reproduction by Rival Colour Ltd, UK
Printed by Craft Print Ltd, Singapore

This book can be ordered direct from the publisher at the website www.anovabooks.com, or try your local bookshop.

Distributed in the United States and Canada by Sterling Publishing Co., 387 Park Avenue South, New York, NY 10016, USA

Page 1: **Mood Swings**
(detail)

Pages 2 and 3: **Spread Your Wings**
210 x 220cm (14 x 88in)
(Photo: Ray Vine)

Left: **Medieval Strippy** (detail).

Opposite: **Long and Thin** (detail).
Leslie Morgan.

Contents

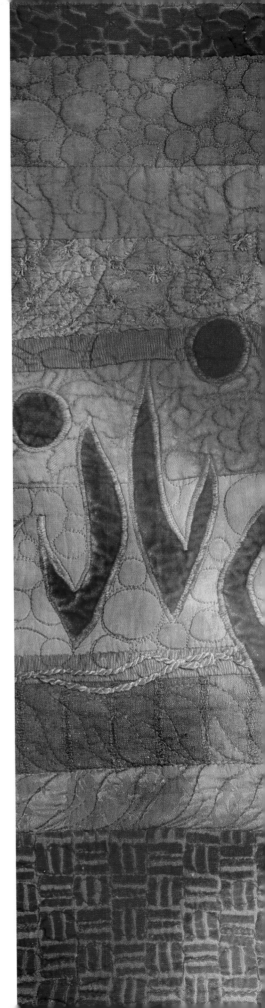

Introduction

'Stitching to Dye' began the way most discoveries do, as the result of a happy accident, which then became a conscious decision and choice in my work. I made a strippy quilt for the Red and White challenge at the Festival of Quilts in 1999, which was staged at Lord's Cricket Ground. When I rinsed the quilt (*Medieval Strippy*) to remove quilting design marks, the colour in the red silk ran into the white and I was faced with a ruined quilt. To salvage the situation I dyed the quilt purple, hoping that this would repair the damage and rescue the piece. The result was not as expected. The blue dye in the purple mix did not register because I had removed the quilt from the dye prematurely, being afraid that the hot dye bath I had used would shrink the wool batting in the sandwich. It did not shrink or felt, and so I over-dyed with blue and was bowled over by the result.

Following this accidental success Leslie Morgan and Colin Brandi suggested that I repeat the experience – doing it 'on purpose'! As a result I started working with natural-fibre fabrics and dyeing the finished pieces. The results were very exciting and generated a flurry of pieces, trying out various combinations of fabrics and colour.

Leslie is an expert in the field of dyeing and generously taught me techniques that I have used ever since, specializing in dyeing stitched layers. For a while we worked in collaboration, 'joining forces', and spent many stimulating hours exploring the possibilities of this process. I am grateful to Leslie for her contagious enthusiasm, encouragement and support, without which I would not have had such an exhilarating adventure.

We particularly liked the texture of the washed and dyed quilts. We tried various ways to exaggerate this texture by using a variety of woollen products, including wool battings, blankets, wool lawn and wool viscose felt. The latter two gave the best results, and this led me to start investigating the possibilities of using these materials to encourage shrinkage.

In the natural progression of things I used a wide variety of fabrics and found that the weight of the cloth had a dramatic effect. Heavier fabrics slowed down the shrinking process; lightweight fabrics gave no resistance, allowing maximum rates of shrinkage. When used alongside one another the contrast in shrinkage rates produced irregular surfaces that I found especially exciting. The next step was to introduce other materials that gave maximum resistance to the shrinkage, such as metal, nylon wire and plastic. The results generated further experiments in dimension and texture which I hope you will enjoy exploring for yourself.

Left: **Joining Forces 1**
approx. 120 x 120cm (48 x 48in)
This quilt was the first one I made with the intention of dyeing it afterwards. It was dyed in a mixture of Magenta and Blue Violet Procion dyes. The colours split, resulting in them both revealing themselves.

Right: **Medieval Strippy** (detail).

Personal statement

The pursuit of happiness is a great motivator. To achieve it we seek various goals, only to discover that happiness still eludes us. Perhaps we are misguided as to what constitutes happiness and spend our lives looking in the wrong place!

I find happiness and am lifted when I work with cloth, creating stimulating stitched surfaces. I am lucky to have the ability and opportunity to spend time doing something that gives me such a buzz. That others wish to share and enjoy what I have achieved is a bonus.

I started stitching early, exploring many avenues along the way. Discovering patchwork and quilting in the early 1990s introduced me to 'stitchery' beyond dressmaking, and I began a voyage of discovery that has kept me stimulated and satisfied ever since. Every aspect of this journey has been fruitful, leading me to where I am now in my textile work.

I do not need a label to describe what I do. We tend to name, file and compartmentalize everything, but by doing so we put up barriers, create rules and restrict activities. How often do we ask if something is 'allowed'?

I believe we need to work freely, that there should be no constraint in our choice of materials and techniques. We do not need the risk of others condemning us because we are 'breaking rules'. Boundaries are frustrating and labels restrict development; the only penalties are the disapproval and condemnation of those who are less adventurous.

I work under the umbrella of 'textiles'. My work is a dialogue within the language of textiles. I create stitched layers, embracing aspects of patchwork, quilting and embroidery, incorporating mixed media, dyeing and embellishing. My works do not claim to be deep and meaningful or aspire to be 'art'. I would like them to be accepted for what they are – stitched, decorative wall hangings which are purely and simply blatant indulgences and expressions of texture and colour. I hope that they give pleasure to others. They bring pleasure and happiness to me!

Left: **Baroquen Spell**
102 x 104cm (40¾ x 41½in)
This quilt was cut back, appliquéd and dyed about six times to achieve the desired depth of colour.

Below left and right: Palm fronds offer inspirational colour arrangements.

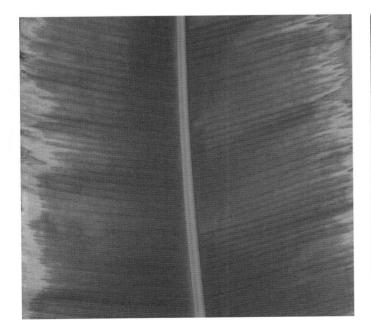

Inspiration and Motivation

My curiosity is what motivates me; I want to know what will happen if I do something differently. What I see around me inspires me. Colour, shape, pattern and texture are everywhere. We are surrounded by sources of inspiration – nature, architecture, art, clothing, magazine illustrations, building yards, garden centres, shop displays – the list goes on and on.

- Look and you will see.
- Ask yourself how you can express what you see with textiles. The answers often come at unexpected times, at two in the morning or on the way to do the grocery shop.
- Act on them; nothing is gained through doing nothing. Take risks and don't be afraid of failing – very few things are real failures. They are only called that because they do not live up to our often unrealistic expectations, or because they fail to achieve success in competitions. Be flexible, accommodate unexpected results and make the most of them. And then – if something is really bad – bin it!

What is innovation?

Where do new ideas come from? How do we know that these 'new' ideas are new? What is innovation? Novelty and originality spring to mind. But do such things exist? How often do you make a discovery, only to find that someone else has also had the same 'new' idea? When this happens I feel oddly cheated and disappointed that my original idea turns out to be someone else's as well.

Perhaps there are no new ideas. Most things have been tried before in one way or another. What makes the new idea unique or innovative is our individual interpretation of it. Innovation arises when ideas are recycled and given a fresh approach – pushing the boundaries a little further. I call it 'the splat syndrome', the dropping of an idea into our thought processes, and then allowing it to splat – spreading out into all sorts of nooks and crannies until it lands on fertile ground and springs into action.

Following instructions is (usually) easy, reproducing what someone else has done before. It is more challenging and satisfying to take that idea and turn it into something that is uniquely your own, an individual interpretation of an idea that incorporates your personal history of techniques and experience.

Discoveries are made in many ways. For me asking the question 'What if?' (my curiosity) and then embarking on experimental work to find answers (there will be more than one), usually turns up results that can be used in subsequent projects. Not all are worth following up, but elimination is also important. What doesn't work this time may well be appropriate at a later date!

The experimentation that leads to discovering answers to my questions generates a very special excitement. The start of a new journey can never be repeated, and in presenting this book I am perhaps denying you the chance of making these discoveries for yourself. However, I hope that you enjoy sharing my explorations and that the path I have suggested will inspire you to try the ideas yourself, finding your own answers and bringing a personal slant to the processes. There are no right or wrong answers, only variations on a theme, each offering an opportunity for personal exploration and development. Your results will vary from those shown because there are so many variables involved, including different washing machines, water temperatures, colour choices and measurements. I see this uncertainty as a good thing, which can only add variety and individuality to the work you produce.

Inspiration can be found everywhere. Carry a camera and photograph interesting surfaces, patterns and shapes that catch your eye.

Individual Development and Progress

The following diagram illustrates a typical learning pattern. Start at the bottom left-hand corner. Before beginning a new learning experience we are unconsciously incompetent – unaware of not knowing. We become consciously incompetent once we start learning something new – we know that we don't know as we embark on our apprenticeship. As we progress and complete our learning we become practitioners – consciously competent. We know that we know. If we persevere and explore what we have learnt to its conclusion we become unconsciously competent – we no longer have to think about what we are doing. We become a master of the process.

Not everyone perseveres until they reach the level of master. Many are content to be practitioners, attaining this level of competence and staying there, happy to be comfortably, consciously competent. Some never leave the apprentice stage, content to add numerous areas of basic expertise to their repertoire, but never taking any particular subject to its conclusion. Others keep building their level of competence to that of master in new aspects of their work, exploring new skills and areas of proficiency by repeatedly working through the learning cycle. The result is that they are always progressive, fresh and stimulated and never allow themselves to stagnate.

Wherever you find yourself in this cycle is a good place to be. The most thrilling place to be is at the beginning, because ahead of you lies excitement and discovery!

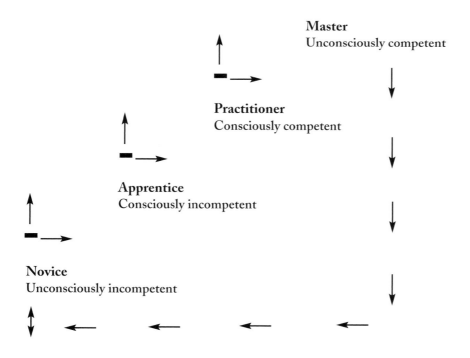

Master
Unconsciously competent

Practitioner
Consciously competent

Apprentice
Consciously incompetent

Novice
Unconsciously incompetent

Opposite: Stimulating surfaces surround us – look and you will see inspiration all around you.

Using this Book

Stitching to Dye is about using mainly white, cream, pale or neutral fabrics of natural fibre content to create textile pieces, which will be dyed when finished to add colour. The whole process is very much about chance, accident and surprise, and is perhaps not for the faint-hearted! It is stepping into the unknown – the results, especially in the beginning, are unpredictable. There is an element of risk involved but taking the plunge is exciting. Being less precious about work and accepting the sometimes surprising results is often difficult, but the reward is liberation. Making the most of what happens and learning at each step of the journey is an enjoyable process – trust it!

The aim of this book is not to give instruction for basic stitching, piecing, patchwork, quilting, embroidery or dyeing. A level of experience and competence in these disciplines is assumed. There are many books available to provide information on techniques you may be unfamiliar with and some of these are listed on page 126. Where techniques are peculiar to an exercise, instruction and explanation are given.

Each reader will use this book and the techniques in a way that is compatible with his or her own work. For an embroiderer the exercises will provide wonderful surfaces for subsequent stitch and embellishment, as is evident in the work in the Shrinkage Gallery (pages 106–119). Patchworkers may find it opens up avenues they had previously not imagined exploring. Techniques used in the Stitching to Dye exercises would translate well into everyday textile work, using coloured fabric and not dyeing. The shrinkage exercises could also be executed with coloured fabric, excluding the dyeing. Textile artists working with mixed media may be stimulated by the possibilities of shrinkage.

The modern trend is to want the quick fix; we want instant results and success. However, taking time over something, savouring the moment and enjoying the process has a lot to offer. The Stitching to Dye process cannot be achieved instantly. It is necessary to take time to learn, and each step is progress towards that superb piece that warms the heart and lifts the spirit. Time and effort are needed, but it will work best if you enjoy the process and love what you do.

I have outlined an action plan which will help you achieve good results. Like all new ventures you will get the best results if you put in some research and preparation at the beginning. The more you know about the materials and processes you are using the more successful you will be. The degree of success depends on dedication and hard work. This book will enable you to:

- Familiarize yourself with the fabrics and threads to use, enabling you to make informed choices.
- Learn about the dyes, chemicals and dyeing processes used.
- Discover how the combination of fabric choice and dyeing will interact by working through some preliminary investigations.
- Consider some basic stitching and quilting techniques.
- Work through the exercises, which fall into two categories: Stitching to Dye (starting on page 46) and Shrinkage (starting on page 78).

The pieces made are not intended to be serious works of art but casual pieces serving as tools of discovery. *Bon voyage!*

Left: **Lighter Shade of Pale**
100 x 127cm (40 x 50in)
This quilt was left undyed. It uses the same design as *Baroquen Spell* on page 8.

Preparation

Being armed with information about the processes and materials involved is important. Disasters and disappointments can be avoided by making some preliminary investigations, thus ensuring pleasing results when working on your first Stitching to Dye project. You will be able to make some educated guesses, instead of plunging into the unknown.

However, if you do not like making systematic explorations, and if you are not too precious about your samples, then there is no harm in 'winging it' – making discoveries as you go along, thus building up personal knowledge through trial and error. This is, after all, largely how I worked through the process myself – learning as I went along.

It can be daunting to add colour to a pure and beautiful piece such as *Lighter Shade of Pale* (page 14). For this reason start by making small pieces or samples, no bigger than 60cm x 30cm (24in x 12in), which will enable you to learn from the results before embarking on larger, more important projects. These smaller pieces are ideal for making bags and book covers.

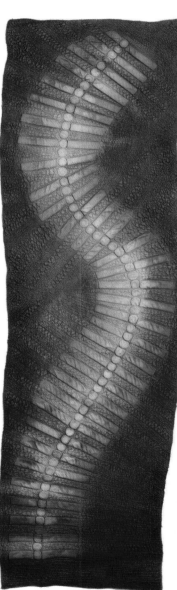

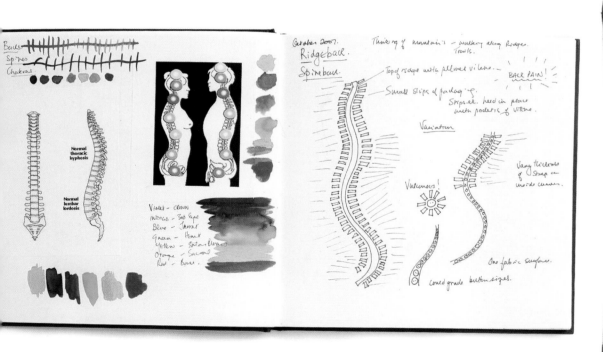

Right: Spine Tingling
33 x 110cm (13¼ x 44in)
This piece was inspired by the
sketches in my notebook, above.

Keeping records

Documenting your research is very important. There is nothing more frustrating than looking at a piece of work and not knowing how you achieved the result. We always think we will remember but very few of us do! So take the time to make notes and catalogue the results. Take photographs of the work, before and after washing and dyeing, and keep them in a scrapbook to remind you of what you did. Your notes and pictures will also help to explain why some things happened, enabling you to repeat or avoid the process in future dyeing projects.

An A4 (11½ in x 8½ in) sketchbook is ideal. Choose one whose pages are strong enough to have samples stuck onto them. Make notes of your investigations, the fabrics you used, the threads, measurements and the sequence of events. Jot down any questions that spring to mind; these will provoke exploration and produce further discoveries.

A scrapbook can expand into a journal, keeping track of your journey, your curiosity and your progress. The more you get into the habit of noting your thoughts and jotting down ideas, the more you will find to record. The journal can be a private place and I find that other areas of my life creep into it. This is not surprising, as what we do in textiles is usually influenced by what else is going on in our lives. It is all part of one big picture, the whole of our existence.

Above: **Spine Tingling** (detail).

Equipment and Materials

The following items may not be in a standard 'toolbox', and are in addition to the usual sewing and dyeing paraphernalia.

GENERAL
- Notebook, sketchbook or similar
- Record cards for storing samples
- Glue gun – useful for mounting pieces on canvases

STITCHING
- Sewing machine feet:
  - darning/quilting foot
  - open-toed embroidery foot
  - zip foot

THREADS
- Water-soluble thread
- Fine thread such as Aurifil 50, DMC 50, Superior Thread, MasterPiece, YLI Machine Quilting Thread

NEEDLES
- Jeans/denim needles 70 or 80
- Twin needle 2.5/80

DYEING
- Litre containers to hold dye solutions
- Turkey basters
- Cat-litter or similar trays, for example those used in gardening
- Plastic bags or bottles for sample work
- Barrier cream for skin

SUNDRY
- Rubber suede brushes (for 'de-fluffing')
- Rubber gloves
- Small sieve
- Small spoons

EMBELLISHMENT
- Markal (Shiva) Paintstiks
- Gold and silver leaf
- Embossing powders, texture gels

Opposite: **Bottlescape** (detail). Markal (Shiva) Paintstiks were used to add a subtle sheen to the surface of this piece.

Below left and right: Dyeing and painting equipment.

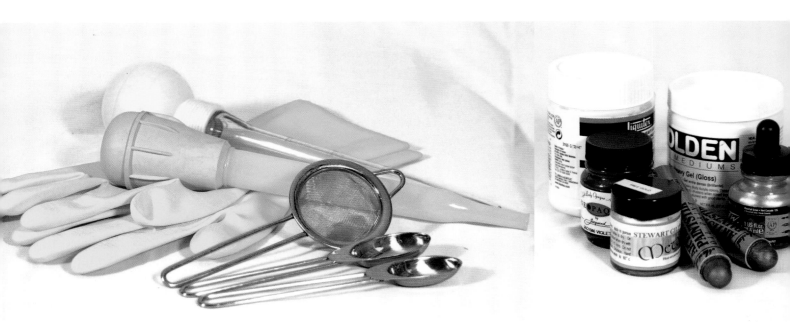

Fabric

There are fabrics of many different weights, structures and fibre types. They can be fine or coarse, thick or thin, heavy or light, textured or smooth, transparent or solid. Fabric can be woven, non-woven or knitted. Most of the cloth I use is woven. Woven fabric consists of two sets of threads – the warp running along the length and the weft running across the width. The weave can be simple, such as in sheeting, flannel and denim, or complex, such as in velvet, damask, towelling and corduroy. The fibre content can be either natural or man-made. Natural fibres in turn are made either from plants, composed of cellulose, or from animals, composed of proteins. Man-made fibres include:

- Regenerated natural fibres such as Tencel, viscose rayon, cellulose acetate and cellulose triacetate.
- Synthetics, such as acrylic, polyester and nylon.

The Procion MX dyes used for the Stitching to Dye exercises in this book are suitable for cellulose natural fibres such as cotton, linen, viscose rayon, jute, ramie or any combination of these fibres. They also work on silk, which is a protein fibre. They are not successful on other protein fibres such as wool, which needs an acid dye. Neither do they work on most man-made fibres, although if the man-made fibre is blended with a cellulose fibre, for example in polyester-cotton blends, they will dye the cellulose in those blends. Tencel and viscose rayon are the only man-made fibres that dye with Procion dyes as they are made from wood pulp.

Assemble a collection of suitable fabrics to use, collecting as many different natural-fibre textiles as possible. Look at all sorts of weaves, such as corduroy, towelling, velvet or jacquards. Select mixed fibres that have a high natural-fibre content; those with too much man-made content will not dye well. Visit charity shops and rummage through their linen baskets and clothing racks for interesting natural-fibre articles. There are many variations in cotton. For example in *Hanging on the Wall 3* (opposite) all but two of the bottles are cotton and each bottle uses a different fabric.

Left and right: A selection from the wide range of silk fabric available.

Contrast

There is a danger when working 'blind' with pale or neutral colours of there being very little contrast, resulting in the work looking a little flat.

Consider the following to create contrast.

Fibre content can make a big difference. Some fibres take the dye very well, resulting in darker colours. Viscose in particular loves dye and gives intense colours when dyed.

The fabric's **thread count** will also make a difference to the depth of colour after dyeing. Closely woven cotton poplin will appear darker than loosely woven cotton muslin.

A **mixed-fibre** fabric will dye differently than those that are 100 per cent of one fibre. If a fabric mix includes either wool or man-made fibres they will dye a paler colour than those of mixed natural fibres.

Pre-dyed or **synthetic coloured fabric** can be used to create contrast.

Below: **Hanging on the Wall 3**
140 x 95cm (56 x 38in)
I used a wide variety of cotton fabric for this wall hanging: cotton fabric was used for all but two of the bottles, and each one is in a different type of fabric.

Fibre identification

The content of some fabrics can be established by sight or feel, but the most certain method is through a burn test. As a general rule, if the burn test leaves a small amount of soft, fine, powdery ash, or beads that crush down to ash, then the fabric will dye with Procion MX dyes. The exception is wool.

Exercise extra care when working with fire. Work in a well-ventilated room, away from flammable curtains or other risks. Working at the sink over a metal tray such as a baking tray kept especially for the purpose is advisable. Equip the tray with a small candle, matches or a lighter and a pair of long-handled tweezers or clamps.

Never burn a corner of a large piece of fabric. Cut a sample, approximately 1 x 5cm (½ in x 2in) from the fabric. Fix this into the clamps and hold it over the lighted candle flame. Be careful as synthetic fibres can flare up quite vigorously (which is why you should test on a small piece of the fabric) and emit nasty fumes. If this happens, release the sample, allow it fall into the metal tray and let it burn out. Do not touch it. Wait for the residue to cool before examining the results.

If you think that the fabric is a blend, separate the warp from the weft and test the fibres separately.

Establish whether the fibres burn or melt and whether they burn quickly or smoulder. Observe what type of flame is produced, what the smoke looks like and the smell given off. After burning is finished, the type of ash or residue left helps establish the fibre content.

Natural fibres such as cotton, linen, Tencel and viscose burn quite quickly (unless treated with a flame retardant), producing a yellow flame, grey smoke and a smell like that of burning paper. The residue is a small amount of soft, fine, powdery ash. Wool and silk burn slowly and irregularly, producing a grey smoke. The smell is like that of burning hair or feathers. The residue is a brittle ash, forming beads that crush down to ash between your fingers. The way to distinguish wool from silk is often by feeling the cloth before you burn it – wool is usually hairy.

Man-made synthetic fibres all melt, usually burning fairly fast, giving off black smoke. The residue is always a hard, uncrushable bead when cool.

Left: Equipment used for testing fibres.

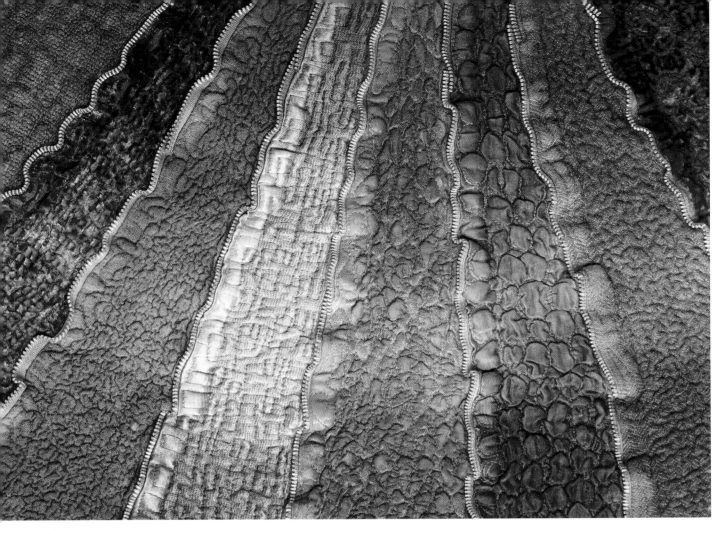

Above: **Mood Swing** (detail).

Fabric preparation

As the work will be washed after it has been finished, pre-washing the fabric is unnecessary. Some fabric is supplied PFD (prepared for dyeing), but most are not. Upholstery fabrics may have been given special treatments that affect how they dye. It is best to scour these first.

SYNTHRAPOL (METAPEX 38 LIQUID)

Synthrapol, also known as Metapex 38 liquid, is a very concentrated and efficient liquid detergent used for cleaning (scouring) fabrics and yarns before dyeing or printing, and as a soaping agent after printing or dyeing processes. Cross-staining of surplus dye onto adjacent fibre (particularly white) after dyeing is a problem that Synthrapol is designed to help prevent. A warm rinse after dyeing followed by a treatment with Synthrapol at 60°C will remove unfixed dye and keep it emulsified to prevent cross-staining.

SCOURING

Scouring with Synthrapol (see above) and soda ash (see page 34) will remove sizing. Wash the fabric as follows:
- Load fabric into washing machine (don't over-fill).
- Sprinkle in 3 to 6 tablespoons of soda ash and ½ teaspoon of Synthrapol for a full load of fabric (about 6m/6yds). The amount depends on the type of fabric – a fine silk will need less soda ash and Synthrapol than a heavy-weight cotton.

Threads

Because of subsequent dyeing, the colour of the thread used is not permanent. This applies to natural threads such as cotton, silk or viscose. If you want a thread to stay the same colour after the dyeing process, use polyester or other man-made thread. This means that the choice of thread colour is flexible and can be made bearing the following in mind:

1. Visibility while stitching: using a just off-white thread on white or cream fabrics means you can see it more easily while stitching.
2. Depth of colour after dyeing: white thread will give you the purest colour after dyeing, pale colours such as beige will turn out slightly deeper.
3. Contrast of colour: using stronger-coloured threads will result in darker versions of the dyed colour. Using man-made fibre threads means the colour will stay the same; using black thread will give a strong contrasting line. Variegated thread offers an interesting effect on the finished piece.

It is also interesting to think of contrast in terms of thickness when selecting a thread. With this in mind, consider threads that can be used in different ways:
- Stitched through the needle with anything up to a 12-weight thread
- Bobbin stitching with a thicker thread in the bobbin
- Couched
- Hand-stitched

The cotton count system (30, 40, and 50) refers to the number of 840-yard hanks of yarn it takes to weigh one pound – the more hanks, the thinner the yarn. This means that thicker threads have lower numbers, so 30 is thicker than 50.

Standard cotton thread is 50/3 (three ply of a 50-weight thread) but not all threads have the thread thickness and ply printed on the label. For fine background quilting or stippling, you need to use a finer thread such as Aurifil 50/2 (two ply of a 50-weight thread). This stops the work becoming hard and stiff. The closer the stitching, the thinner the thread should be.

For bolder lines use a thicker thread such as a 28, 30 or 40 weight thread.

NEEDLES

Thicker needles have higher numbers; thinner needles have lower numbers. 90/14 is thicker than 70/10.

For crisp stitching use sharp needles such as Jeans/Denim, quilting 70/10 or 80/12 or embroidery 75/11. For metallic or thick threads use a special needle such as a Metallica or Topstitch 90 needle; these have bigger eyes to accommodate thicker, bulkier threads.

Above: A selection of threads and cords that can be used in your work.

Opposite: Different weights of cotton thread were stitched on a white fabric, and the resulting sample was then dyed to see the outcome.

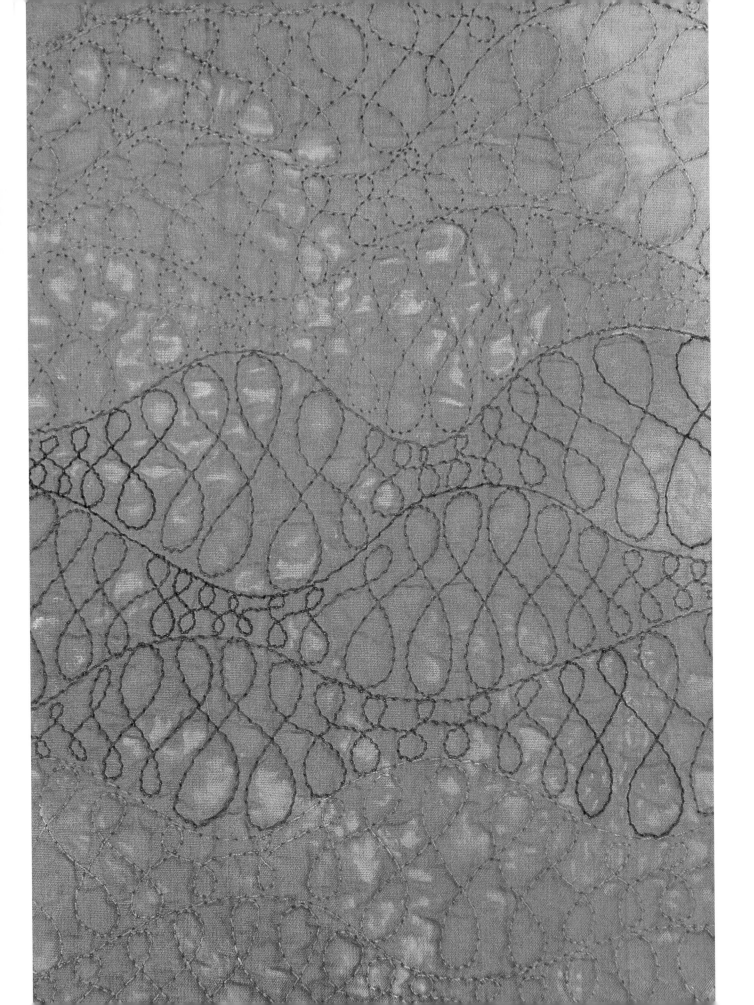

Stitch

Stitch plays a very important role in the Stitching to Dye process. The samples and examples in this book are layered in the quilting tradition with a top layer, a layer of batting and an optional backing. Primarily, the purpose of the stitch is to hold the layers together, but there are secondary functions such as texture, pattern and embellishment.

Either hand or machine stitch, or a combination of the two, is suitable. I have used free-machine stitching for the samples, with hand stitch being used mainly for embellishment. The stitching is more visible on the Stitching to Dye pieces, but once shrinkage is introduced, stitch creates predominantly texture and surface pattern; most intricate stitching or quilting will not be visible after shrinkage.

The question 'How *should* I quilt it?' always arises. Replace it with 'How do I *want to* quilt it?' or 'how do I *need to* quilt it?' and your approach will be different. There isn't a single answer and the possibilities are endless. There is no right or wrong way, but some will work better than others on a particular project. **Please yourself** – if it works for you then that is good enough. Above all, develop a sense of excitement, pleasure and happiness in the process. Turning it into a chore negates the purpose of the whole creative process!

Look around you for inspiration – a pattern can be inspired by the spiral on a shell, the pattern on a drain cover, oil droplets on a serving dish or ripples in the sand on a beach.

When considering the quilting of a piece, note that:
- Stitch shows up best on plain and solid-colour fabrics and lines are lost on busy prints.
- When dyeing, white or pale cotton thread used on white fabrics will dye with the fabric, creating texture. Coloured or synthetic threads are needed to emphasize line.
- Quilting needs to relate to the quilt; it needs to belong.
- Stitch can be fatal – don't kill the work! The loft of the batting offers the opportunity to create contrast between stitched and unstitched areas. Hammering the whole piece with dense stitch will flatten it and the batting may as well be left out.
- The eye needs areas of repose and reflection. To quote the poem *Desiderata*: 'Remember what peace there is in silence.'

Look at the following areas for inspiration or starting points:
- **Character** or the **style** of the quilt. Stitch can convey emotion: it can be calm, chaotic, angry or hot, for example.
- **Theme** carried by images and words.
- The **fabric** often has patterning or texture that can be emphasized by stitching around it.

Questions to ask

- Is there a focal point? Are there areas to which you want to draw attention?
- Can natural elements be used, such as repeat patterns or shapes in the blocks?
- Can movement or direction be created or emphasized?
- Is more contrast needed? How can this be achieved?
- Are there large, plain areas that would benefit from quilting designs?

Piecing

Working with fabrics other than cotton can be tricky. Stitching lightweight fabrics to heavier ones, working with unstable, slippery cloth and piecing velvet can all pose problems. Use a lot of pins with difficult fabrics and stitch slowly. Special care is needed when working with velvet as the pile shifts. Thorough pinning and reducing the pressure of the pressure foot helps. Try free-machining velvet seams if your skills are up to it. If all else fails the fabric can be stabilized with lightweight fusible interfacing.

Free-Machining

General tips

If you haven't yet tried free-machine stitching, don't be afraid of it. Enjoy the process of learning a new technique and aim to enjoy the process in comfort, with pleasure and no stress. There is no deadline or competition, so don't race. Be relaxed and have a positive attitude. Your mental attitude counts – stress and anxiety will create tension and discomfort.

Make your work area comfortable, allowing your body to work in a relaxed way without causing aches and pains afterwards. When machining, use your hands and fingers, not your arms. Let your hands feel relaxed – gripping the work too hard just increases tension, so try aids such as gloves. The height of the machine bed should be at the level of your elbows when they are bent at 90° – about waist high. An adjustable chair helps. Because tables and chairs are usually designed to achieve this position, placing the sewing machine onto the table raises the work surface about 10-12cm (4-5in); now raise the chair to the right level. If your feet are off the ground as a result, consider having a box or platform for the foot pedal or use a specially designed cabinet.

Speed is something that you need to sort out for yourself. This is not a race – 'foot flat on the floor' isn't necessary. The speed you work at is personal to you, so do not worry about how fast or slowly other people work – find your own speed. Start off slowly and build the speed up as you find your comfort zone. Stay in control. Adjust the speed with which you move the fabric to suit the speed of the machine. Running the machine fast and moving the work slowly results in tiny stitches. Running the machine slowly and moving the fabric fast produces long stitches. Somewhere in between is the point at which the stitches will start being even and recognisable. The trick is not to worry about the length of the stitches – as you become more experienced at free-machining, they will fall into place.

Below: Free-machine stitching.

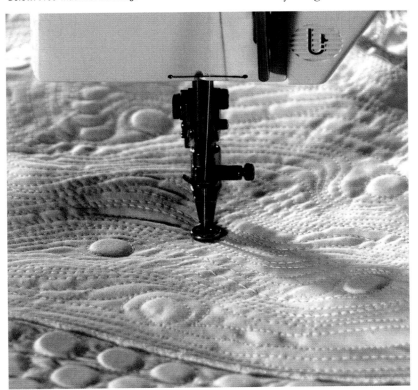

Make speed adjustments according to the intricacy of the work – when following lines, concentration is necessary, so slow down the movement of your hands, but also slow down the machine speed! Free-machining with no lines to follow requires less concentration and you can speed the machine and your hands up. Whatever you do with one, do with the other. If you start running the machine faster, move the work more quickly. If you slow the machine down, slow your hands down.

Generally speaking, look ahead – not at the needle. You will end up doing a combination of both but be aware of the space that you are working into – this way you will avoid getting into tight spots. Anticipate and adjust your working speed accordingly.

To summarize:
- Enjoy the process.
- Remind yourself that it won't be perfect first time round. It takes time to perfect.
- It is OK to make mistakes. Watch babies – they tumble many times before they are able to walk.
- It is OK to cross lines – unless you are doing meandering or vermicelli stitch which requires you not to. There are other options.
- Be kind to yourself – every practice session will show an improvement.
- Breathe!
- Think breast stroke, not doggy paddle. Tiny hand movements will result in tiny stitches.
- Don't race – be in control and gradually build up your speed.
- You are not in a competition.
- Good enough is perfectly acceptable.
- You can't make a circle out of four stitches – for small patterning in stippling, smaller stitches will be needed.
- Use finer thread for close working.

Opposite: Possible patterns for background stitching.

Below: Detail from an untitled piece by Ingrid Press containing stitch patterns.

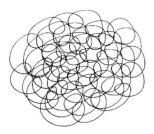

Above: Granite stitch.

Opposite top: **Baroquen Dreams** (detail). Granite stitch is used to create shading and contrast. Photographer: Robert Claxton.

Opposite bottom: Possible patterns for background stitching.

Right: **Verdigris** (detail). Granite stitch is used to secure appliqué edges in this piece.

Granite stitch

Familiarize yourself with this stitch in preparation for use in some of the exercises. Granite stitch is a series of tiny circles, overlapping each other, almost entirely covering the background. It is mostly used for close filling and shading.

Prepare the machine for free-machine stitching and stitch in a circular movement, overlapping circles to cover the background. Keep the circles quite open for a stippling stitch as shown in fig 1 (left). For shading and filling make the circles smaller, overlapping them more densely as in fig 2 (left), as seen in the detail of *Baroquen Dreams* (opposite). Use a finer thread or a rayon embroidery thread when stitching this densely, as a normal-weight thread will result in very stiff work.

Granite stitch can also be used to secure the edges of appliqué, giving a soft, flexible edge. Work circles along a line of stitching as seen in figs 3 and 4 (left) and the detail of *Verdigris* (below). Stitch firstly along the appliqué stitch line, then double back in a circular movement to form a circle into the applied fabric (fig 1). Return, stitching along the line and extending the stitches one circle's length beyond the first circle; then double back again to form the next circle. The stitched edge of the appliqué is reinforced and the circles go into the applied shape, effectively securing the edges of the appliqué. Practice will achieve small, regular circles as in fig 4.

Note that you cannot achieve a circle with four stitches! Stitches need to be small.

CORDED PIN-TUCKS

Soft gimps and cords – knitting cotton is ideal – can be stitched to the underside of fabric using a twin needle. Use a pin-tuck presser foot or one with a hollow underside.

Some machines have an extra hole in the stitch plate to thread the cord through in order to guide the cord. Others use a special attachment fitted to the stitch plate. Use a twin needle (you will need two threads on top) and select a cord that passes through the cording hole or guide comfortably and that runs smoothly between the twin needles. Thread the cord through the hole or guide and pull it to the back of the machine, laying it under the pressure foot. As you stitch, the cord will automatically lie directly in between the two lines of stitching and be secured to the underside of the fabric with the bobbin thread.

If your machine doesn't have either of these facilities, a piece of drinking straw taped onto the machine bed in front of the needle works well. This also enables the use of cords too thick to go through the hole or guide – the twin needle used must be wide enough to accommodate the thicker cord.

TWIN-NEEDLE WORK

The maximum stitch width to use with a twin needle fitted is the widest stitch width of your machine less the width of the twin needle. Engage the twin needle lock on your machine if it has one. You cannot pivot on the needle when a twin needle is fitted.

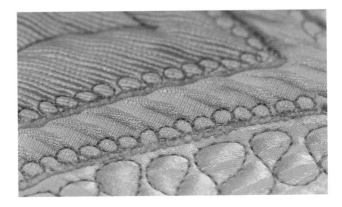

Dyeing

There are many different dye recipes. I encourage you to refer to books about dyeing for specialized information (see Further Reading, page 126). The methods I am suggesting are those I have developed for use when dyeing layered and stitched work.

HEALTH AND SAFETY PRECAUTIONS
Handle dyes with care – they are especially dangerous in powder form when they can easily be inhaled.
- Wear gloves and protective clothing. Use a skin barrier cream on your hands before you put the gloves on.
- Avoid inhaling the dye powder and vapour – wear a mask as a precaution.
- Use only implements and utensils set aside for dye work when mixing and storing dyes and chemicals.

Procion dyes

I use Procion fibre-reactive MX dyes. Although Procion MX dyes are called 'cold water dyes', they are best used at a temperature of around 50-70°C. Do not mix them with very cold or boiling water, and use them warm. The dyes will last for approximately three days when mixed in a salt solution. After this time the strength is reduced. If soda is added to the mixture it will only last for approximately 1–3 hours.

Using six primary colours produces a wide range of secondary colours. For example, Lemon Yellow mixed with Magenta will result in a bright, sharp orange, whereas mixing Golden Yellow with Scarlet gives you a warmer, richer orange. Mixers or blenders such as Red Brown (Brown Rose), Rust and Charcoal add to the repertoire. Dyes without MX codes are mixed by the supplier. Those with MX codes are either pure colours, or mixtures prepared by the manufacturer. Choose according to the MX code. Names given to colours vary from supplier to supplier. The dyes suggested in the table opposite are those I use most. Explore other available colours.

	Colour	Suggested Procion Code
Cold Primaries	Lemon Yellows	Yellow MX-8G *also* Yellows MX4G, MX6G Mixture - MX-G
	Magenta	Red MX-8B *also* Red MX-5B
	Turquoise	Turquoise MX-G
Warm Primaries	Golden Yellows	Yellow MX-GR *also* Yellow MX-3R
	Scarlet	Red MX-G *also* Red MX-3G
	Blue Violet	Blue MX-7RX *also* Blue MX-R and MX-G
Other useful colours	Browns	Red Brown MX-5BR Tan Brown MX-GRN Dark Brown MX-3G Mustard MXR Kemtex 'Reactive' Rust CD
	Black	Kenactive Black K2647 Black MX-CWA
	Green	Olive Green MX-G
	Charcoal	Kemtex Reactive Charcoal CD

Left: Samples of fabric dyed with the
dyes I use most – top to bottom
Lemon Yellow, Golden Yellow,
Turquoise, Blue Violet, Magenta,
Scarlet, Rust, Red Brown (Brown
Rose) and Charcoal.

Splitting dyes

When I first dyed pieces (*Joining Forces 1* and *Medieval Strippy*, shown on pages 6 and 7) I discovered that using mixed dyes resulted in both colours revealing themselves. For both these quilts I mixed a purple dye bath using Blue Violet and Magenta, resulting in a mixture of the two colours. Dyes that are mixed colours will split if the soda ash is added early on and the fabric not moved to even out the strike. This happens because the colours that are in the dye recipe strike at different speeds. The result is that silk, cotton and viscose strike different colours.

Chemical ingredients

The same ingredients are used for all processes – Procion MX dyes, soda ash, salt and urea.

Soda ash (Sodium carbonate) is the fixative necessary to generate the chemical reaction that fixes the dyes to the cloth. It can be obtained from swimming pool-supply companies (sold as Alkali pH Plus) or from specialist dyeing suppliers. It is not to be confused with household soda, which contains caustic soda as an impurity and this can cause dulling and weakening of shades.

Salt encourages the dye molecules to move around the fibres, driving the dye into the fibres, making it more efficient. The amount of salt in a dye solution is relative to the amount of dye used. More dye, more salt. There are dye recipes that exclude salt, especially for low-water-immersion dyeing. I have found that better results are achieved when salt is included in the recipe. However, Ann Johnston's method of low-immersion dyeing without salt, using plastic bags, outlined in her book *Color by Accident* (see Further Reading, page 126), works well.

The salt requirements for the methods used are detailed separately with the process instructions.

Urea increases the solubility of the dyes in water and enhances the brightness and intensity of the dyes used. It is hygroscopic, serving as a humectant, or water-attractor, retaining moisture even when dried, and this boosts the colour yield of the dye during the fixing stage. Urea is not necessary when dyeing in large quantities of water. The processes used are wet enough not to need a wetting agent; many dye recipes exclude urea.

I use a small amount of urea when mixing more stubborn dyes to help dissolve them. Using hotter water and mixing well also works. Too much urea can make it harder to dissolve some dyes. Experiment and come to your own conclusions.

Opposite: **Darker Shade of Pale 1** (detail).
This piece was dyed with Charcoal Dye,
a dye mix that splits.

Right: **Havana Split** (detail).
This foundation-pieced sample was dyed in
MX Havana Brown, a mixed dye that split on
the different fibres.

Dyeing methods

There are many ways to add colour to the finished work. The three main methods described in this book are:
1. High-water-immersion dyeing – submerging the piece in a bucket of dye solution.
2. Low-water-immersion dyeing, where the dye solution is applied directly to the surface.
3. A combination of these two – first dyeing with one colour, followed by direct dyeing.

Dyeing in a washing machine

Larger pieces are often easier to dye in the washing machine. Commercial dye products especially designed for this process are available.

Fabric paints can also be used to colour the work, but this method is not covered here. They generally need to be fixed with heat which is not always practical with layered work. I have had success with both thick and thin Procion dye paint mixes. Refer to the books listed on page 126 for more information on related techniques. Acrylic and other paints can be used but need a fabric medium to fix them to textiles.

Immersion dyeing in a bucket

This method is best suited for pieces that will fit comfortably in a bucket. Larger pieces are more difficult, sometimes resulting in air pockets and unsightly blotches of colour where work has folded, and are best dyed flat or in a washing machine.

Weigh the piece to be dyed – dry weight. Calculate the quantities of dye, soda and salt needed for the weight (see below). Wash the work using a small amount of Synthrapol (no fabric softener or detergent) before adding it to the dye bath. The work needs to be damp when added to the dye.

SALT FOR BUCKET DYEING
More water is involved when immersion dyeing in a bucket and the amount of dye used is relative to the weight of the piece to be dyed. The following table is a guide to the required proportions of dye to salt and fabric weight. Weigh the piece to be dyed to establish the quantities to use.

Below: Dye in tubs.

Weight of work in grams	Dark strength DYE in grams	Dark DYE in tsp	SALT in cups	SODA in tbsp
100	4	1	1/2	2
500	20	5	2 1/2	10
Weight of work	Med. strength DYE in grams	Medium DYE in tsp	SALT in tbsp	SODA in tbsp
100	1	1/4	2	1 1/2
500	5	1 1/4	10	7 1/2
Weight of work	Pale strength DYE in grams	Pale DYE in tsp	SALT in tbsp	SODA in tbsp
100	0.2	0.05	1 1/2	1
500	1	0.25	7 1/2	5

Right: Low-immersion dyeing in a tray in progress. Top: **Test Case 1**. Bottom: **Test Case 2**.

PREPARING THE DYE BATH
- Put about half a cup of hot (not boiling) water into a 1 litre (1¾ pint) container.
- Add and dissolve 1 tsp of urea in this water (optional).
- Mix the dye powder into the water or water/urea mixture.
- Fill the container with hand-hot water and mix thoroughly. Strain through a fine sieve to remove any lumps.
- Some stubborn red dyes and mixes need very thorough sieving to prevent little red spots appearing on the work.
- Add the salt to a bucket and dissolve with 2 litres (3½ pints) of hot water.
- Add sufficient warm water to accommodate the piece to be dyed.
- Add the dissolved dye to the bucket and mix well.

PROCESS
- Mix the required amount of soda ash and set aside for later.
- Add the work to the dye bath and agitate for about five minutes. Squeeze out any bubbles and ensure that the piece is thoroughly soaked in the dye. You can keep the quilt from 'popping up' above the water level by adding a weight to the surface – another bucket with water in it works well.
- Agitate and stir frequently to ensure that the colour is evenly distributed.
- After the work has been in the dye for 20–30 minutes, lift it out of the water with one hand and add the mixed soda solution to the dye bath. Lower the work back into the dye.
- Leave it in the dye for an hour or more, agitating frequently.

RINSING
Rinse the work well to remove any excess dye. Dye left in the work can oxidize when dried, leaving unsightly dark marks.

Wearing gloves, drain off all the dye solution and rinse the work in cold water repeatedly until most of the dye has been removed. Do a final hand rinse in warm water, adding a few drops of Synthrapol.

Transfer the piece to a washing machine, and run the rinse cycle with **a very small amount** of Synthrapol. **Do not** use too much of this rinsing aid as it will froth up and cause flooding from the washing machine. Follow this with a machine wash at 60°C using some more Synthrapol.

When the wash is finished lay the work out on a flat surface to dry.

Low-immersion dyeing

With this method the dye is applied directly to the damp work. Colours are added where you want them. Soda ash is not added until you are satisfied with the colour arrangement.

The dye is blended into the layers as it is added, easing out any blotches and tide marks. Because the dye is being poured onto layers of fabric and batting it doesn't rush around as it would on cloth, so there is time to blend the colours as required.

1.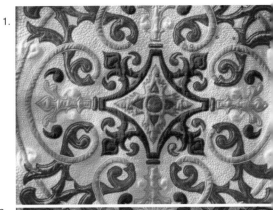
2.
3.
4.

Left: Progressive steps in the dyeing of **Verdigris** (detail). See page 45 for finished piece. 1. The stitched quilt, using pre-dyed fabric, ready to be dyed. 2. The quilt was first dyed with Blue Violet dye using bucket immersion dyeing. 3. The quilt 'stewing' in a tray after low-immersion dyeing. 4. The final result.

SALT FOR LOW-IMMERSION DYEING

The following table is a guide for mixing dyes used in immersion dyeing. Generally I mix dyes to a medium strength for direct dyeing quilts, preferring to dye the piece a few times to get the intensity of colour I want.

Dye strength	Salt to 1 litre of water
Strong – 2 tsp of dye	500 grams (1lb 2oz)
Medium – 1 tsp of dye	250 grams (9oz)
Weak – ½ tsp of dye	100 grams (4oz)

I use generous rounded or heaped teaspoons, not precise measurements. This varies with the dyes used – red dyes (Magenta and Scarlet) are aggressive and dominant, so less is needed. Warm and cool yellow dyes are less aggressive; both need up to 50 per cent more dye powder.

PREPARING THE BASIC PRIMARY COLOURS
- Pour about half a cup of hot (not boiling) water into a 1 litre (1¾ pint) container.
- Optional – add and dissolve 1 tsp of urea in this water.
- Add the required amount of dye powder to the water or water/urea mixture and mix.
- Make up to 1 litre (1¾ pints) with salt solution and mix well.
- Strain the mixture through a fine sieve a couple of times to remove any lumps. Some stubborn red dyes and mixes need very thorough sieving to prevent red spots.

PROCESS
Prepare a soda solution of three heaped tablespoons of soda ash to 1 litre (1¾ pints) of water. If the quilt is a large one make up a few litre tubs.

- Place the damp work in a suitable tray. If it is too large for a tray, use a plastic sheet laid on a smooth hard surface such as a patio.
- Lay any threads or backing fabric alongside or under the work.
- Using turkey basters, cover the work with dye solution as required.
- Gently blend the colours into one another with your gloved hands. Take your time and make sure that the whole work is covered with dye.
- Leave to 'stew' for 20–30 minutes.
- Add the soda solution using a turkey baster, taking care to saturate the whole piece.
- The longer you leave the piece to fix after adding the soda the better. Three hours or more is best. If left overnight make sure that it is kept damp – drying out results in oxidisation, leaving marks on the surface. Cover it with plastic sheeting to prevent this.
- Pour out the dye and squeeze as much liquid out as possible.
- Rinse as for immersion dyeing in a bucket.

Dye can be added again immediately if required, or you could wait until the work is dry to see if more dyeing is required.

LEFT-OVER DYES
Wet a piece of washed fabric and put it into a bucket. If there is too much liquid in the tray when you are dyeing, pour some off over the fabric. At the end of a dyeing session pour left-over bits of dye over the fabric as well – the results are often remarkable pieces of cloth.

Using colour with the direct application method

Colour can be used in a number of combinations. A good colour wheel for reference is very useful. Colour schemes most commonly used are:

Monochromatic – using only one colour, for example *Tangoed* (page 47).

Analogous – combining several colours sitting next to one another on the colour wheel, for example yellow, orange and red as in *Pathways* and *Fire in my Soul* (pages 95 and 101)

Complementary – using colours which are opposite one another on the colour wheel – see blue/orange, purple/yellow and red and green as in *Ancient and Modern* (page 58).

You will gain valuable information from the results of the first steps – see Testing and Exploring on page 42. When dyeing stitched layers, try:

- Using a single colour – an alternative to immersion dyeing. Large pieces are often difficult to accommodate in a bucket. Dyeing these flat has the advantage of controlling blemishes and preventing air pockets. Stunning effects can be achieved by mixing different strengths of a primary colour and grading from light to dark.
- Using only two primary colours (analogous or complementary) is the safest way to move on. There are two of each, giving four dyes to play with. Mixing the warm and cold primary colours will give a good variety of secondary colours. Golden Yellow with Scarlet will give a different orange than one created by blending Lemon Yellow with Scarlet. Mixing a secondary colour with the two colours being used can help with blending.
- When you have grown accustomed to the results of combining two primaries, try introducing the mixers – especially Brown Rose and Rust. Black and Charcoal need to be handled with care. Again, experimenting with colour mixing on fabric is well worth the time. Combine three primaries with extra care – mud is always lurking to pounce! Introduce a third primary cautiously, little bit by little bit. Experiment by mixing secondary colours and adding small amounts of the third primary, or a complementary colour. A third primary can be added to the work if it is applied in rows of colour so that there is always a blended edge of only two primaries.

There are many more possibilities to explore and many books available on the subject.

Colour arrangements

The colours can be arranged in the work in various ways.

- Radiating colour from the centre – start with a pale colour in the centre of the work, then arrange other colours in bands around the centre, radiating to the edge.
- Merging two colours from opposite ends of the piece.
- Stripes – horizontal, vertical, diagonal – bands of colour in rows across the work.
- Swirls of colour merging into one another.
- Random – apply the colour in a random way, merging colours into one another as in a flower garden.
- Three different focal points of colour – start with three areas of colour – these could be the same, for example all golden yellow, or turquoise, blue violet and a mix of the two. Draw other colours into these, blending to create radiating colours.
- Specific to each section or block of work. If the work is block-based use the same colour combinations in each block.

Opposite: Colour wheel made from images of flowers and vegetation.

Testing and Exploring

Before you start work, it is always worth doing some preliminary investigations to find out what sort of fabric you are dealing with, and how you can expect it to behave.

FIBRE-CONTENT TESTING

When the fibre content of fabric is unknown, take a small sample of the fabric and carry out the burning test as explained on page 22. Stick a piece onto a small index card, keeping a card for each fabric. Further dyeing investigations carried out on the same fabric can be added to this card. Note your findings and identify the fabric. Other information can be recorded on the card, for example where the fabric was bought and its price. The cards can be filed alphabetically, perhaps arranged in sections by fabric type, for easy referral. Alternatively use a page in your scrapbook, leaving space for further samples. A small price tag is a useful way of labelling the main piece of fabric.

COLOUR TESTING

Mix up dyes into jars, cut small samples of washed fabric (identify with a permanent marker), dye, dry and document on cards.

SAMPLING THREADS

Stitch a small sample with threads, note for identification, dye and document conclusions.

COLOUR MIXING

Investigating the potential of the Procion MX dyes by carrying out an exercise in colour mixing is a valuable step towards understanding what will happen when you start adding dyes to your finished projects. By combining the six primary dye colours only once, with one another, results in 15 different secondary colours:

	BV	TQ	SC	MA	LY	GY
Blue Violet	1	7	8	9	10	11
Turquoise		2	12	13	14	15
Scarlet			3	16	17	18
Magenta				4	19	20
Lemon Yellow					5	21
Golden Yellow						6

- You need a number of small containers – bottles or small plastic food bags.
- Mix up base stock of all the dye colours that you will be using. Do not add soda to these dye stocks so that you can continue the exercise over a few days.
- Mix up 1 litre (1¾ pints) of soda solution (3 tbsp to 1 litre [1¾ pints] of water).
- Choose a good white cotton fabric ready to dye – poplin or sheeting are good choices. Cut this up into pieces approximately 5cm to 10cm (2in to 4in) square. (You could work on larger pieces, building up a stash of dyed fabric, keeping a sample from each piece for your records. Adjust the dye quantities accordingly.)

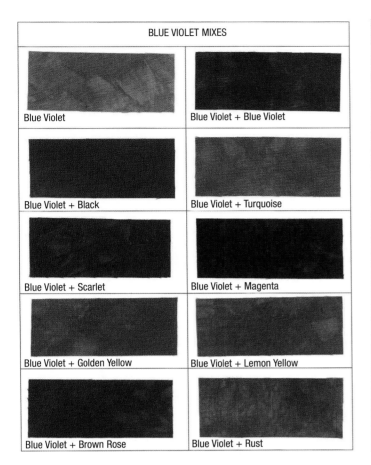

BLUE VIOLET MIXES	
Blue Violet	Blue Violet + Blue Violet
Blue Violet + Black	Blue Violet + Turquoise
Blue Violet + Scarlet	Blue Violet + Magenta
Blue Violet + Golden Yellow	Blue Violet + Lemon Yellow
Blue Violet + Brown Rose	Blue Violet + Rust

GOLDEN YELLOW MIXES	
Golden Yellow	Golden Yellow + Golden Yellow
Golden Yellow + Blue Violet	Golden Yellow + Turquoise
Golden Yellow + Scarlet	Golden Yellow + Magenta
Golden Yellow + Black	Golden Yellow + Lemon Yellow
Golden Yellow + Brown Rose	Golden Yellow + Rust

Above: Colour record cards.

- Place a piece of fabric into each plastic bag or container. Start with one piece for each of the dyes that you have mixed – at least six primaries.
  - Using a turkey baster or measuring jug, pour enough dye into each container or bag to cover the fabric. Make a note of the quantity and be consistent with this measurement.
  - Allow the fabric to lie in the dye for 20–30 minutes and then add a squirt of soda mixture and agitate well.
  - Leave for at least a further 30 minutes.
  - Rinse, wash and dry the fabric. Iron the samples and stick them onto a record card, documenting the colour and any other useful information such as times or quantities.
  - You will have samples 1 to 6 in the table.

SECONDARY COLOURS

Work your way through the primary colours, mixing each one with each of the others in equal parts. Work one colour at a time – the number of pieces you produce will decrease with each colour processed.

- Place a piece of fabric in five containers or bags.
- Select the first primary colour in the table, Blue Violet, and label each of the five containers or bags Blue Violet.

- Add the name of the five other primaries to the labels, ending up with five labels:
    1. Blue Violet + Turquoise
    2. Blue Violet + Scarlet
    3. Blue Violet + Magenta
    4. Blue Violet + Lemon Yellow
    5. Blue Violet + Golden Yellow
- Pour half the quantity of Blue Violet dye used in the first phase of dyeing into each container.
- Add the same quantity of dye from each of the other primary colours according to the label.
- Complete as for the first round.
- You will now have samples 7 to 11 in the table.

Continue the exercise with each of the remaining primary colours. With each new colour the number of samples is reduced by those already mixed.

If you have included the mixer dyes mentioned on page 32 the table would end up with 45 samples in addition to the pure dyes/colours.

	BV	TQ	SC	MA	LY	GY	BR	R	Ch	Blk
Blue Violet	1	11	12	13	14	15	16	17	18	19
Turquoise		2	20	21	22	23	24	25	26	27
Scarlet			3	28	29	30	31	32	33	34
Magenta				4	25	26	37	38	39	40
Lemon Yellow					5	41	42	43	44	45
Golden Yellow						6	46	47	48	49
Brown Rose							7	50	51	52
Rust								8	53	54
Charcoal									9	55
Black										10

Further explorations

You could expand this research by varying the ratio of the colours mixed – instead of a ratio of 1:1 you could try 1:2. Try a combination of three colours, or, if you have dyed larger pieces, colours could be overdyed with one another. You would end up with hundreds of samples, but you would have an invaluable collection of colours for reference.

Opposite: **Verdigris**
90 x 93cm (36 x 37in)

Stitching to Dye

The following exercises are intended to serve as samples rather than projects. The sequence presented here will allow you to explore the Stitching to Dye potential most effectively. Following the suggested plan will help you achieve new knowledge and understand the possibilities, making fabric choices easier and clearer in the subsequent explorations.

If you have carried out the first steps of testing and exploring you will have established how fabrics and threads react to dyeing. Referring to your notes and samples will make fabric choices easier and more effective.

Record your findings and especially make notes of any 'what ifs…?' that arise. Move forward from those findings, incorporating the discoveries made. If 'mistakes' are made, or the results are not pleasing or as you had hoped, do not beat yourself up – learn from the experience, using the information to advantage in further exercises.

Whenever marking is required, always check that the pen you use will wash out before using it. I use a water-soluble pen but always rinse the work in cold water before washing.

If the results lead to diversions from the path mapped here, follow those diversions! They will always result in valuable answers.

When assembling layers use either safety pins or temporary spray, as preferred. Finish edges of samples or projects however you like: by bringing surplus backing fabric to the front, binding the edge, overstitching or trimming to leave a raw edge.

*(**Please note** that directions for the suggested exercises do not always include detailed instructions for construction techniques unless these are new and peculiar to that exercise. A general knowledge of basic patchworking and piecing is assumed).*

Opposite: Details of log cabin-style quilts dyed in different colours. Clockwise from top left: **Red Alert**; **Joining Forces 1**; **Silk Centred**; **Tangoed**; **Blue Rinse**; **Magenta Magic**.

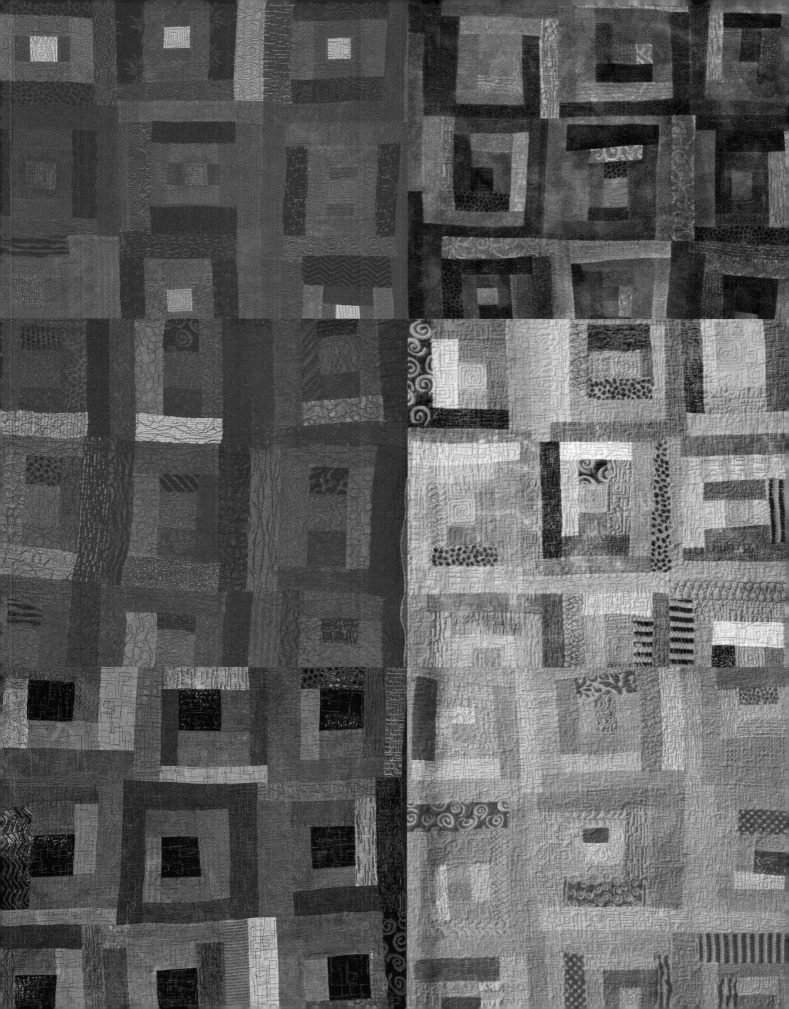

Exercise 1
Taking the first steps

REQUIREMENTS
- A selection of white, cream or pale natural-fibre fabrics
- Cotton thread
- Cotton batting
- Cotton backing

Make a small patchwork sample using a variety of natural-fibre fabrics (white, cream or pale). Any block could be used. Log cabin is perfect as there are endless variations without complicated and precise piecing. Blocks can be precise and accurate, with regular-width logs, or more informal using logs of irregular width in themselves, or strips varying in width from one another. Fabric choices could be constant, making identical blocks as in *Finding Your Feet* (opposite), or random as in *Blue Rinse* on page 47.

As the piece will be dyed in a bucket or a tray using a single colour, restrict the size to a maximum of 1 metre (39 inches) in any direction.

GUIDELINES
- This is the first step of the journey – do not agonize over it, just get on with it!
- Use any knowledge gleaned from the preparatory exercises to make informed choices.
- How the blocks are constructed is not important, but using a variety of fabrics is – this experimentation gives the opportunity to learn their potential for future projects.
- Use a selection of at least eight fabrics when constructing the blocks.
- Choose a variety of fibre content and texture, referring to samples dyed in your colour-testing exercises for guidance.
- If you do not know the content of a piece of fabric, test it to avoid disappointment.
- Use cotton thread to piece and quilt.
- Use a cotton batting and backing when assembling the sample.

When finished, wash and dye the patchwork sample following the instructions for basic immersion dyeing in a bucket (see page 36).

Below: **Blockhütte** (detail),
Clever use of fabrics in this quilt has created a lively variety of log-cabin blocks. Ingrid Press.

Opposite: **Finding Your Feet**
84 x 84cm (33½ x 33½in)
This log-cabin piece was dyed in Violet Navy MX-4RD, a mixed dye that split on the different fibres.

Exercise 2
Including pre-dyed fabric for enhanced contrast

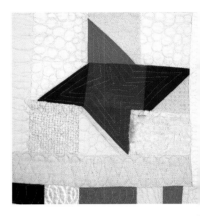

The ability to anticipate the outcome when dyeing will come with practice. In the meantime pot luck will rule, with more educated choices being made as you progress.

Secondary colours and contrast can be introduced by including pre-dyed or coloured fabric in the construction. When over-dyed, the pre-dyed fabrics will produce colours not available with one-colour dyeing. Yellow fabric when over-dyed with blue will give greens, or, over-dyed with red, produce orange. Pre-dyed red fabrics were included in *Roaming in the Gloaming* (opposite), which was over-dyed with Kemtex Reactive Charcoal CD.

Any construction technique is suitable. *Roaming in the Gloaming* was made using improvized or liberated piecing. Initially this can be difficult, but an enormous sense of freedom is achieved once you have learnt to 'let go'. Inspiration came from African-American quilts that were made using paper templates, resulting in irregular and quirky-looking pieces. The process described here is perhaps a little contrived, but the results are pleasingly informal!

Beware – in exercises 2 and 3 coloured or black fabric used may run, so use a colour catcher when washing. **However,** if the colours do run, the problem will be remedied when dyed.

REQUIREMENTS
- A selection of white, cream or pale natural-fibre fabrics
- Pre-dyed fabric to introduce contrast and new colours
- Cotton thread
- Cotton batting
- Cotton backing

TIPS FOR LIBERATED PIECING
- Use a ruler with no measurements marked, or try to ignore the markings.
- Do not cut pieces too small.
- Do not unpick – if pieces go in the wrong way, leave them.

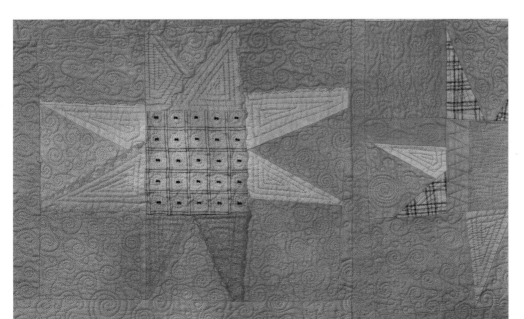

Above: Red dye blocks, before and after dyeing. Don't panic if the colours run – dyeing usually fixes the problem.

Left: **All Stars** (detail)
A quilt constructed using liberated piecing. Ingrid Press.

Opposite: **Roaming in the Gloaming**
74 x 104cm (29½ x 41½in)
Red pre-dyed fabrics were used to add contrast in this quilt.

PROCESS

1. Choose one or two traditional blocks as a starting point. Make a rough diagram of these for reference.
2. Decide on the approximate size of the blocks and of the final project, for example six blocks. Blocks do not have to be square.
3. Use the pre-dyed or coloured fabrics for emphasis in every block.
4. **Without measuring**, cut pieces for the blocks.
5. Join these in a logical sequence, making up smaller units of the block (fig 1). Where edges to be pieced are not straight, lay them together and trim along the seam edge with a rotary cutter and ruler.
6. Join these smaller units into rows (fig 2). Do not worry about the points not meeting or being cut off.
7. Trim to straighten the edges of the rows (fig 3) to make joining them into a block easier (fig 4).
8. Add strips to two sides and trim to a right angle on the corner where they meet (fig 5).
9. Add strips to the other two sides and trim to a right-angled block the required size (fig 6).
10. When all the blocks have been pieced, assemble them as required. If the blocks are irregular in size, make them equal by adding extra strips of fabric.
11. Add a border, sandwich and quilt.
12. Wash and dye as desired – the sample was dyed in a tray using only one colour.

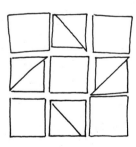

Fig 1 Make up smaller units of the block.

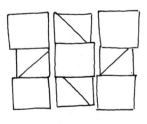

Fig 2 Join these smaller units into rows.

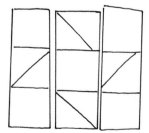

Fig 3 Trim the rows to straighten the edges.

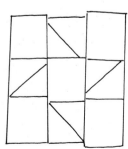

Fig 4 Join the rows into a block.

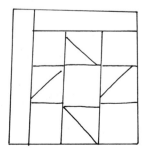

Fig 5 Add strips to two sides and trim to a right angle.

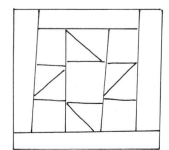

Fig 6 Add strips to the other two sides and trim to form a right-angled block.

Opposite: **Tarantaal** (detail). Tarantaal is the Afrikaans word for guinea fowl. Photograph: Peter Woodall.

Exercise 3
Introducing printed black-and-white fabric and incorporating lace and other embellishments

REQUIREMENTS
- A selection of white, cream or pale, natural-fibre fabrics
- Black-and-white printed fabric
- Cotton thread
- Cotton batting
- Cotton backing
- Lace trimmings – consider materials such as rickrack, lace fabric including black lace, Broderie Anglaise, crochet or knitting. Test content to make sure it will dye!

Assemble a patchwork top approximately 60cm x 30cm (24in x 12in), incorporating the black-and-white printed fabric to create interest and contrast. Include plain black fabric such as dupion silk and silk noile.

Overlay, insert or piece lace. If using lacy fabric, consider laying a piece of interesting fabric underneath (viscose satin or similar) which will shine through after dyeing.

When the sample has been assembled, sandwiched, quilted and washed, dye it as follows:

First step – dye the piece in one colour in a bucket or in a tray, choosing a medium strength of one of the primary colours.
Second step – once rinsed and washed, lay the piece in a tray and add dye, using the low immersion dyeing technique.

TIP: Before sandwiching, trim and remove any stray black threads.

The original primary colour can be reinforced and a variety of colours produced by adding other primaries. Avoid using all three primaries in one area to prevent a mud colour, unless mud is what you want!

When the piece is dry after rinsing and washing, consider whether it is necessary to dye it a second time.

Above: **Black and Blue**: assembled block before washing and dyeing.

Below left and right: Detail from **Black and Blue**. Left: Black dye has run into the surrounding fabric. Right: The offending blemishes are no longer visible after dyeing for a second time.

Opposite: **Black and Blue** 72 x 105cm (28 x 42in)

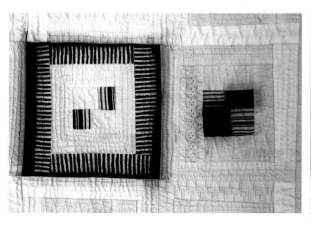

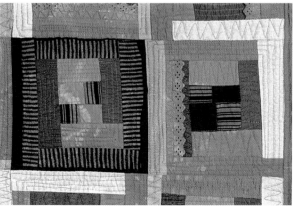

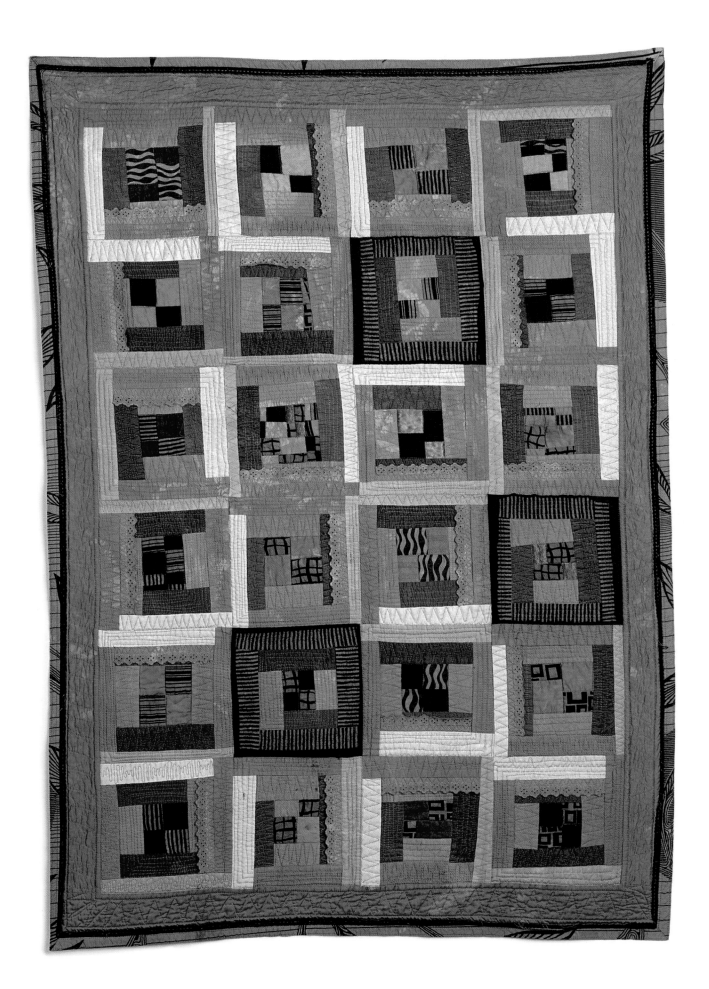

Above: **Birthday Treat**

60 x 67cm (24 x 26¾in)

Opposite: **Hamba Gashle** (detail). Printed black-and-white fabric was incorporated into these two pieces to create interest and contrast.

Above: **Ancient and Modern**

90 x 90cm (36 x 36in). The design of **Verdigris** (page 45) was used to create a piece that combined an ancient design with modern synthetic fabrics. The pattern was applied to a silk background using fabric normally used to make suitcases and rucksacks.

Exercise 4
Introducing synthetic fabric and thread

REQUIREMENTS
- A selection of white, cream or pale natural-fibre fabrics
- Synthetic fabric in a bright colour
- Synthetic thread, such as polyester top-stitching thread
- Synthetic braid or cord – optional
- Cotton thread
- Cotton batting
- Cotton backing

Make up a quilt top using any construction method preferred – pieced blocks, log cabin or stripped. In the planning of the piece consider how to use the synthetic fabric to best effect, bearing in mind that it will not change colour when dyed.

Right: **Lime Zest**
71 x 71cm (28 x 28in)

Exercise 5
Foundation techniques

REQUIREMENTS
- A selection of white, cream or pale natural-fibre fabrics
- Pre-dyed, printed or synthetic fabrics (optional)
- Cotton thread
- Cotton batting
- Cotton backing

Use a variety of fabrics and consider previous discoveries to enhance the work. Include fabrics that suit the elements of the composition, such as fences, pebbles, etc, using the textures and patterning to good effect. Consider mono-printed, stamped or painted fabrics. Strips could be pieced before they are laid down, or texture could be added with stitch or cording. Shapes can be applied after all strips have been stitched in place to complete the piece – see *Skybird* (opposite).

Although this exercise uses strips of fabric constructed in horizontal lines, the sequence of stitching could also be log-cabin or crazy patchwork.

FOUNDATION – STITCH AND FLIP
1. Establish the size of your sample – *Strata* (page 63) was approx. 40cm x 80cm (16in x 32in). Making a rough sketch helps plan the composition.
2. Layer cotton batting onto a cotton backing fabric.
3. Place a strip of fabric on the batting, right side up, at the top end. Stitch to the batting along the top edge.
4. Lay another strip along the lower edge of this strip, right side facing down onto the right side of the first strip. Stitch along the edge through all layers. Flip and press in place. Continue until whole area is covered. Add interest by varying the shapes of added strips. See below for instructions on how to include angles and curves.
5. Add further stitching as necessary, using free-motion techniques and threads of various weights and composition.
6. Consider couching thicker braids or using thicker threads in the bobbin for contrast in the quilting.

CURVES – STITCH AND FLIP
1. Follow steps 1–3 above. Place a cutting board between the batting and the fabric (fig 1).
2. Lay a second fabric alongside the first, overlapping the adjacent edges with right sides facing up (fig 2). Overlap the fabrics enough to accommodate the depth of the required curve.
3. Cut a gentle curve through **both** layers of fabric using a rotary cutter (or scissors if preferred) (fig 3). Discard the two skinny off-cuts from both pieces (fig 4) and remove the cutting board.
4. Draw registration marks or snip 'v' marks on the edges if the curves are quite deep or if the strip is long.
5. Turn the new piece over, laying the curved edges of the two strips **right sides together**.

Left: **Long and Thin** (detail).
Leslie Morgan.

Right: **Skybird** (detail).

Match any registration marks and pin in place, if wished (fig 5). Stitch through the batting and backing as well as the pieces being joined with a comfortable seam allowance, fitting the two edges into one another.

6. Flip and press. Correct any places along the seam where the curve hasn't been stitched deeply enough by stitching along the ironed crease as a guide line.

OVERLAPPING CURVES

Angles or deeper curves not suitable for piecing can be overlapped. Follow steps 1–3 on page 60. After cutting the angles or curves, shift the new piece up under the secured piece, making sure that the overlap is enough to hold the two together. Pin in place and then stitch through all layers to secure. Overlapped selvedge and frayed edges make interesting features (fig 4a).

When finished, dye using low-immersion dyeing in a tray as outlined on page 38, in colours to suit the piece.

Opposite: **Strata** (detail).

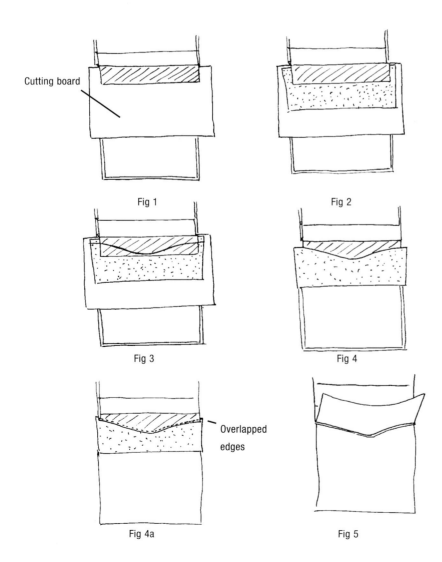

Cutting board

Fig 1

Fig 2

Fig 3

Fig 4

Overlapped edges

Fig 4a

Fig 5

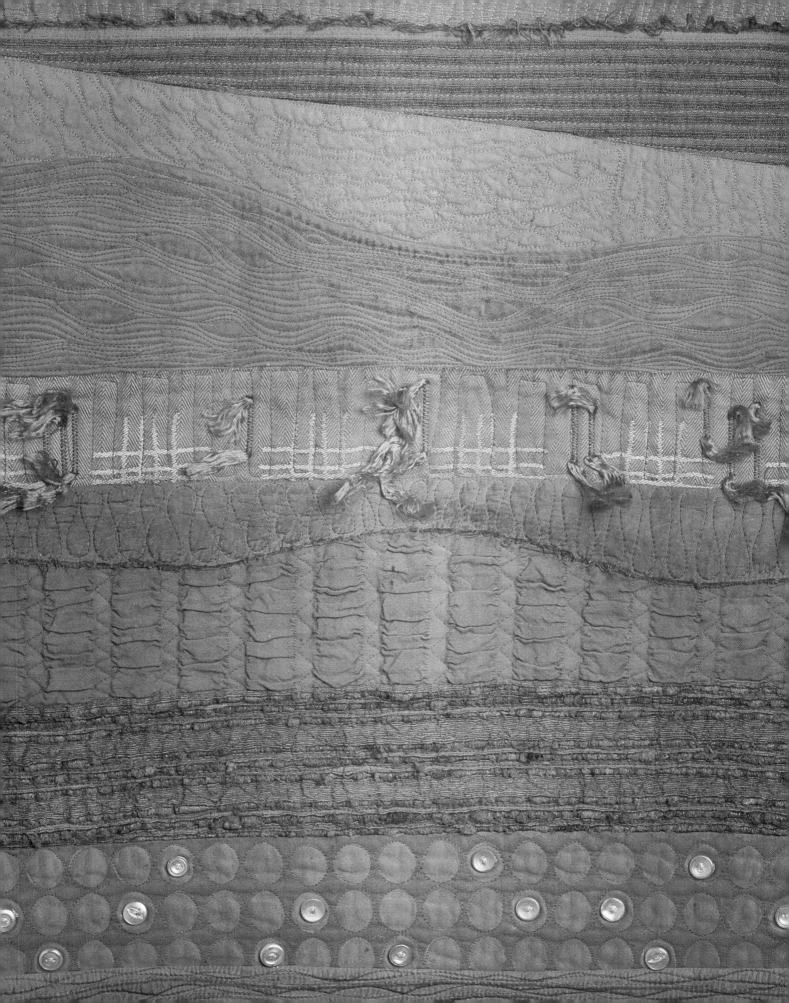

Exercise 6
Appliqué from the front using one fabric

REQUIREMENTS
- Two pieces of fabric with strong contrast when dyed (consider shiny/matt, smooth/textured). One piece is the background, the other will be applied.
- Cotton thread
- Cotton batting
- Cotton backing
- A design suitable for appliqué
- Marking pen
- Small, pointed, sharp scissors

1. Mark the design on the fabric to be applied. Lay this marked fabric on the background fabric and sandwich these with cotton batting and a backing fabric, securing with safety pins on the front.
2. With the feed dogs down, free-machine around the marked shape with small stitches.
3. Trim away the excess fabric around the **outside** of the stitched line, using sharp scissors. Leave a small margin of fabric. **Note**: the applied shapes are like islands on the background.
4. Finish the edges off with granite stitch or an open zigzag stitch.
5. Quilt and finish, then wash and dye following the low-immersion dyeing instructions on page 38.

VARIATION: CUT-BACK
Instead of applying the design, try placing the contrasting layer of fabric underneath the top layer and cutting back through the top layer to reveal the underlying fabric. For maximum contrast between the underlying and the top layers consider shiny/matt, patterned/plain, pre-dyed/un-dyed, textured/plain, and so on.

1. Mark the same design as previously used on the top fabric.
2. Make up a sandwich of the marked top fabric with the fabric to cut through to underneath it, followed by the batting and backing. Secure with safety pins on the front.
3. With the feed dogs down and using small stitches, free-machine around the areas for cutting back.
4. Using sharp scissors, trim away the fabric **inside** the stitched line of the design, leaving a small margin of fabric. **Note**: the design is like a lake or puddle in the background.
5. Finish the edges off with granite stitching or an open zigzag stitch.
6. Quilt and finish, then wash and dye following the low-immersion dyeing instructions.

Right: **Ginkgo Leaves** (detail)
This piece was created using 'slap appliqué'.
Sonia Fox.

VARIATION: SLAP APPLIQUÉ

This technique can be used to build up a surface covered with informal shapes, for example leaves or pebbles. See *Ginkgo Leaves* by Sonia Fox, opposite.

1. Make up a sandwich of background fabric, batting and backing.
2. Draw a shape on a scrap of fabric.
3. Place this on the background fabric and stitch around the drawn line. Alternatively, place the piece of fabric on the surface and stitch the shape freehand.
4. Cut away the excess fabric around the applied shape.
5. Build up the surface, overlapping shapes to fill the whole area required.
6. A double row of stitching would be sufficient to secure the edges, but granite stitch would be more secure.
7. Consider mixing transparent fabrics in with others for added effect.

Right: **Night Flight**
71 x 71cm (28 x 28in)

Exercise 7
Appliqué from the back using multiple shapes, fabrics and colours

REQUIREMENTS
- A selection of white, cream or pale natural-fibre fabrics
- Cotton thread
- Cotton batting
- Cotton backing
- A plain background fabric, cotton batting and backing fabric the same size

TIP: Using a pre-dyed or coloured background fabric helps to create contrast between the applied shapes and the background. See *Hanging on the Wall 2* on page 70 and *On the Shelf,* opposite.

- A suitable design for appliqué
- Marking pen
- Small, pointed, sharp scissors

1. Establish the order in which the parts of the design need to be applied, working from the back of the design (i.e. the images, parts, etc. furthest away in terms of perspective) and number them (fig 1).
2. Mark the design on the backing fabric before assembling the sandwich. Remember to **reverse** the image when marking on the backing.
3. Assemble the sandwich – marked backing, batting and background fabric. If pinning to sandwich, pin from the back.
4. Turn the sandwich over so that the front of the work is uppermost. Lay the first piece of fabric to be applied (right side up) on the **front** of the work. Check that the relevant section of the design is covered by holding the sandwich up to the light, marked side facing you. Pin into place, making sure that corners are out of the way to avoid folding and tucks.
5. Turn the work over to the back so that the design is uppermost. With the feed dogs down, free-machine around the shape covered by the fabric, making small stitches. It is important to stitch around **all** sides of the shape being applied. Areas adjoining one another will be stitched twice.
6. Turn the work over so that the front of the work is uppermost. Carefully trim away the excess fabric around the stitched line of the shape, leaving a small (approximately 2mm/¹⁄₁₆in) margin of fabric, taking care not to snip the background or adjoining pieces. Where shapes overlap, trim a slightly wider allowance on the edge to be overlapped (fig 2). To prevent shapes pulling away from the stitching when applying a loose or open weave fabric, leave a wider margin. It can always be trimmed back later.
7. Continue to build the design up in the same way, using different fabrics as required (figs 3 and 4).

Opposite: **On the Shelf**
56 x 31cm (22½ x 22½in)

8. When all pieces have been applied (fig 5), finish the edges with granite stitching or open zigzag.
9. Quilt as necessary and finish the edges.
10. Wash and dye using the low-immersion dyeing method.

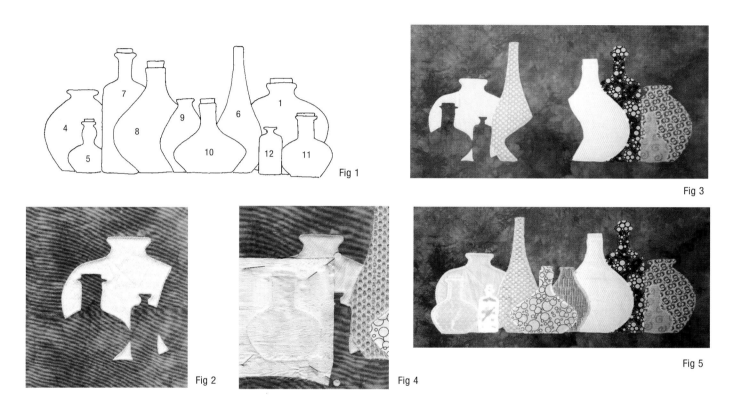

Fig 1

Fig 2

Fig 3

Fig 4

Fig 5

Exercise 8
Combining appliqué with cut-back

REQUIREMENTS
- A selection of white, cream or pale natural-fibre fabrics
- Cotton thread
- Cotton batting
- Cotton backing
- A plain background fabric, cotton batting and backing fabric the same size
- An integrated design using at least three different fabrics – a background, areas to be cut back to and one or more to be applied
- A piece of contrasting fabric to cut through to
- Marking pen
- Small, pointed, sharp scissors

1. Draw the design on the backing fabric.
2. Mark areas of the design that are to be cut back, and the order of the appliqué.
3. Assemble a sandwich with background fabric on top, fabric to cut through to next, followed by the batting and lastly the marked backing. Secure the sandwich with safety pins from the back. **Note**: the fabric for appliqué is not included in the sandwich as it is added at step 7, below. If cutting through to a printed fabric, make sure that it is laid **right** side to the front.
4. Free-machine around the areas for cut-back, making the stitches small.
5. Trim away the background fabric **inside** the stitched line of cut-back areas of the design, leaving a small (approximately ¹⁄₁₆in) margin of fabric (fig 2).
   Note: the cut-back shapes form puddles into the background, and the appliqué forms islands onto the background.
6. Next complete the appliqué following the instructions in Exercise 8.
7. Secure the edges, quilt as necessary and finish.
8. Wash and dye in a tray.

Fig 1

BG = background CB = cut back AP = applied

Fig 2

Fig 3

Above: **Figure of Eight**

30 x 30cm (12 x 12in)

Stitching To Dye Gallery

Left, top: **Hanging on the Wall 2**
125 x 92cm (49 x 36in)
The background fabric in this piece came out of a 'slop bucket' at a workshop. I 'auditioned' pieces of this fabric in the various dye options to see which dye would produce the most pleasing result. Finally, the quilt was dyed in Magenta. This choice determined the colour of the pre-dyed fabric used for some of the bottles.

Left, bottom: **Hanging on the Wall**
105 x 76cm (42 x 30in)
In contrast to **Hanging on the Wall 2**, this piece was made entirely from white fabric. I relied on the take-up of the dye to create contrast.

Opposite: **Hot Flush**
66 x 66cm (26 x 26in)
Another interpretation of the design used for **Verdigris** (page 45), applied from the back and dyed using the low-immersion method (see page 38).

Opposite: **Oxo**
44 x 50cm (17½ x 20in). Jackie Dorkings.

Above: **Moonlighting** (detail)
These two faux-chenille wall hangings were created by layering five to
seven fabrics, then stitching, slashing and dyeing them.

Above: **Autumn Panel**

45 x 45cm (18 x 18in)

Numerous different types of fabric were used to create leaf shapes which were applied before this piece was dyed. Jenny Pudney.

Opposite: **Field of Poppies 1**

45 x 90cm (18 x 36in). Jackie Martin.

Opposite, left: **Darker Shade of Pale 2**

35 x 133cm (12¾ x 33in).

This piece was first dyed with Charcoal and then overdyed with Rust.

Opposite, right: **Ginkgo Leaves**

32 x 83cm (14 x 53in).

This piece was created using 'slap appliqué'. Sonia Fox.

Above: **Celtic Hope**

136 x 136cm (54 x 54in)

The fabric for this quilt was screen-printed with symbols that were present in the black-and-white printed fabric.

Shrinkage

Manipulating texture and distortion

Each of the exercises in this section explores the potential of specific materials as a resistance to shrinkage. Combining the various materials with techniques previously learned will produce amazing results.

Wool is the agent used to implement the shrinkage. A standard quilt sandwich consists of a layer of batting sandwiched between a backing fabric and a top. By replacing the batting layer of the sandwich with wool and washing aggressively in hot water, the wool layer shrinks and creates surface texture.

I use wool viscose felt (70 per cent wool and 30 per cent viscose) and arctic wool gauze. Both are British products. Other woollen stuff such as old blankets and some woven fabrics such as wool lawn can be used, but always test to ensure they have not been treated to prevent shrinkage. Wool viscose felt can shrink up to 25% or more after vigorous washing. Arctic wool gauze (a fine wool gauze similar to a muslin) has the potential to shrink up to 50% but needs repeated washing to achieve this result. Measurements for some worked samples in the exercises taken 'before and after' are in a table in the Appendix (page 125). It cannot be stressed enough that these are intended as a rough guide only. The results relate to one instance, under a particular set of conditions and circumstances. The chances of getting exactly the same results are very slender.

The shrinkage potential is increased by **excluding** the backing fabric. The intensity of the shrinkage will depend on the resistance implemented by the top layer of fabric in the piece. A fine lawn, for instance, will not present much resistance to shrinkage, whereas a heavy denim fabric will.

Doubling the layer of shrinking material **does not** increase the rate of shrinkage – it slows it down, offering increased resistance. However, progressive layering with the shrinking agent after the initial shrinkage will enhance the technique. So stitching onto either felt or gauze first, shrinking and then layering again onto felt or gauze, stitching and shrinking again will give exaggerated results. See *Mixed Metaphors* (Leslie Morgan) and *How can You Laugh?* in the Shrinkage Gallery (pages 106–119).

The rate of shrinkage can be affected and controlled through adding and including materials that resist the shrinkage, slowing it down in certain areas.

Always trim any excess felt or gauze from the outside edge of the work as it will shrink more than the layered and stitched areas and cause unwanted distortion.

Bearding

Like a lot of things in life there is a price to pay for the exciting results achieved with this process. The downside is that wool products are prone to bearding – the migration of wool fibres through the fabric to the surface. This is more likely to happen with wool viscose felt – Arctic wool gauze is less prone. It is most severe when very fine or loose woven fabrics are used. Some wool products do not beard as they have been specially treated, but because of the treatment they also do not shrink, which defeats the object of these exercises.

Opposite: **Un-Zipped** (detail).

I have found no solution to this problem. This means that with most pieces there will be a degree of de-fluffing to be done. In my experience this is best done when the work is wet. Rubber suede brushes and rubber gloves can be useful, but sadly it is often down to a few hours (on large pieces) of plucking to get rid of the bearding.

Try experimenting with acid dye which will add colour to the wool fibres, thus using the bearding to create another dimension to the work by creating a 'shot' look.

Shrinkage Options

Adding materials such as plastic, metal, pelmet Vilene, extra felt or foam to the project will slow down the shrinkage rate of the wool agent in those areas. These materials need to be water-resistant, otherwise they will disintegrate in the washing and dyeing processes.

ADDITIONS

1. **Appliqué:** Apply shapes to the top surface or underside of the fabric. Ensure anything applied to the top surface is suitable for dyeing or otherwise acceptable on the top layer.
2. **Trapunto:** Apply softer material (such as pelmet Vilene, extra felt or foam) to the underside of the top layer. Mark the chosen design on the top using your preferred marker. Lay a piece of the material to be added (big enough to cover the whole of the design) on the underside of the fabric behind the design. Stitch around the shape from the front, turn the work over to the back and trim excess material away.
3. **Bonding:** Plastic and pelmet Vilene may more easily be applied under the top layer by bonding into place with Bondaweb (Wonder Under), fabric glue or temporary basting spray. Once in place the layers are sandwiched together and the shapes stitched around to secure them.
4. **Trapping:** Buttons and flat tapes or shapes can be placed in channels or pockets made of lightweight interfacing, water-soluble fabric or a fine gauze/muslin stitched to the **underside** of the top fabric.

Left: Useful materials to include when shrinking.

Opposite: **Heavily Disguised** (detail). Zips were inserted into the seams in this piece to resist shrinkage and cause distortion.

INCLUSIONS

1. **Seam Insertion:** Include trimmings with an edge that can be stitched into, such as zips, lace or piping cords, in the seams, allowing them to stick out on the front when the seam is opened. A zipper foot is useful for doing this.
2. **Tucking:** Materials with edges that can be stitched into can be tucked into pleats or tucks, for example zips and trimmings.
3. **Enveloping:** Materials with no edge, such as strimmer nylon, string, wire, thick cords or package tape, can be enveloped in a fold, pleat or tuck. You can hold them in place by stitching close to the edges with a zipper or piping foot.
4. **Couching:** Materials such as strimmer nylon, string, wire, thick cords or package tape can be couched into place onto the top or underside of the top layer, whichever suits.

Some extremely distorted results are best mounted to a firm surface such as an artist's canvas for display.

Exercise 1
Shrinkage using stitch only

Note: Wool viscose felt has been used throughout the exercises; substituting Arctic wool gauze will achieve greater shrinkage. Make a provision of 20% to 50% larger than the required finished size, depending on the filling. The finished size cannot be predicted. There are too many variables involved, such as density of stitch, method of washing, temperature, agitation or drying. The shrinkage exercises take you through various options. Although each exercise concentrates on a single material or technique, incorporating these in further explorations will be very effective.

REQUIREMENTS
- Plain white natural fabric such as cotton sateen, silk or silk cotton
- Lots of lightweight threads (MasterPiece, DMC 50 or Aurifil No 50) as this exercise guzzles it!
- Wool viscose felt

1. Make a rough sketch of how you plan to stitch the design.
2. In *Feeling the Heat* (page 84) sections have been allocated for three distinct areas of stitch – a central panel worked with a combination of circles and lines flanked by two side panels of grid work.
3. Transfer this plan onto the fabric, marking guidelines for stitch.
4. The three areas here have been defined by folding the fabric and stitching a tuck or pleat into the fabric. Parallel lines of stitch have been worked into this pleat to flatten and firm it. After the shrinkage this will gather into a frill.
5. Layer the marked fabric on the wool viscose felt and secure with safety pins.
6. Using fine thread in both the bobbin and through the needle, free-machine stitch the design as planned. Keep the stitching simple, as fancy or intricate patterns will be lost when the work is shrunk. Density of stitch is the main contributing factor to the surface distortion. Unstitched areas will bobble up, whilst densely stitched areas will slow the shrinkage down.

GRIDS AND SQUARES
The grid needs to be larger than the finished size – making allowance for the shrinkage – and could be irregular. The greatest effect will be achieved by creating a chequerboard of either stitched and unstitched sections, or densely stitched sections contrasted with other loosely stitched areas.

CIRCLES
Solid: Stitching in a circular motion, filling a circle with concentric rows of stitch banked against each other causes 'cupping' – forcing the area of the circle to peak or cup. It takes a lot of stitch (and a lot of thread) but it does work! It is best to work from the centre outwards – the cupping makes working inwards awkward. Stitching is easier if the cupping is popped to the back of the work once it becomes cumbersome.
Outlined: Stitch rings of solid stitch.

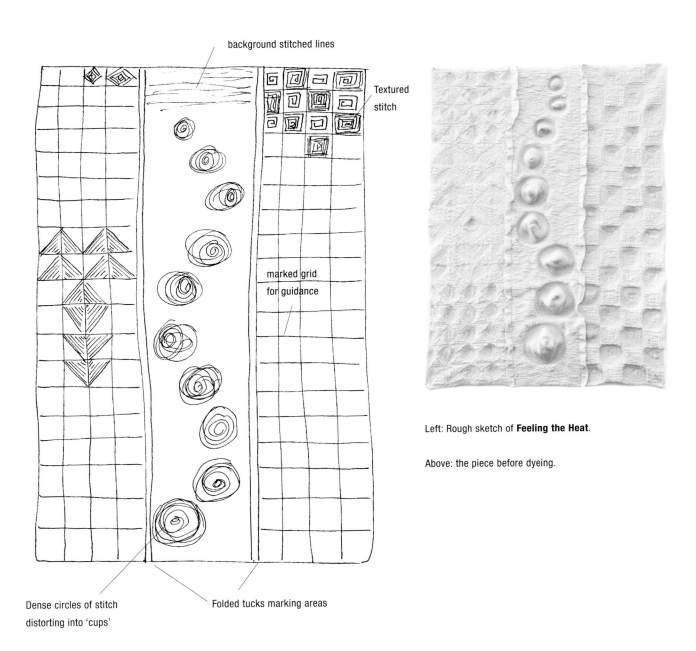

background stitched lines

Textured stitch

marked grid for guidance

Left: Rough sketch of **Feeling the Heat**.

Above: the piece before dyeing.

Dense circles of stitch distorting into 'cups'

Folded tucks marking areas

LINES
Stitch lines of dense stitch with strips of unstitched spaces in between. Lines could be curved, undulating, zigzag or overlapping.

FILLING
Areas can be filled with close stitching such as vermicelli or granite stitch.

7. Wash and dye in a tray following the low-immersion dyeing instructions.
8. Embellish as required.

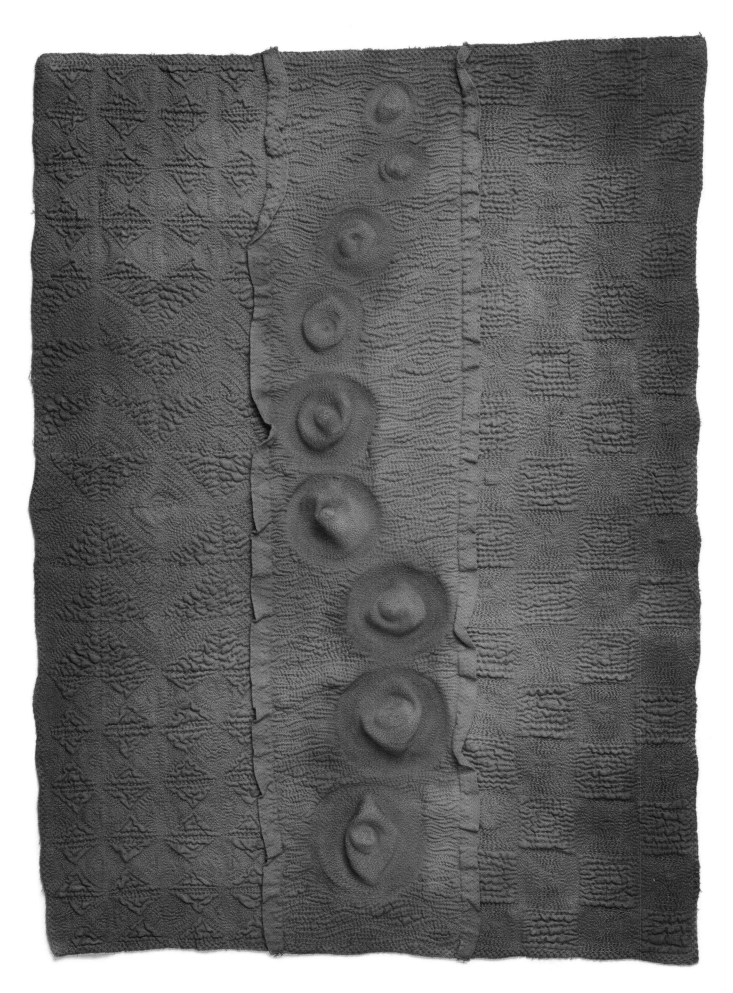

Exercise 2
Using cords or braids

Cords or braids which resist shrinkage, or shrink at a different rate, can be used to encourage undulations, ripples and crinkles, depending on the flexibility of the material.

REQUIREMENTS
- Plain white natural fabric such as cotton sateen, silk, silk cotton
- Wool viscose felt
- Lightweight thread
- Thick cords, braids such as piping cord, viscose cord, synthetic coloured cords or nylon string

OPTIONS
Stitch a grid of needle-corded pin-tucks onto the underside of the top fabric using knitting cotton and a twin needle. Because the cotton is soft and pliable the result is a soft texture. See corded pin-tucking, page 31.

Nylon string was used instead of knitting cotton (see below), resulting in a more distorted texture as the nylon is harder and resisted the shrinkage.

Opposite: **Feeling the Heat**
37 x 53cm (14¾ x 21in).

Below: Using nylon string.

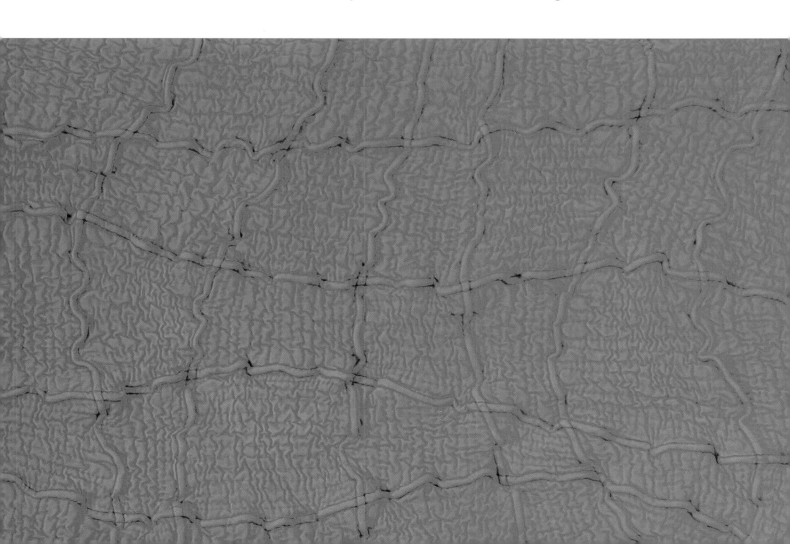

Couch a grid of viscose braid on the top surface through all the layers of fabric, as in *Applied Braids*, below.

In *Grid Lock* and *Glimpses* (opposite) a dense grid of various thicknesses of threads and cords was couched onto a background of Arctic wool gauze. Because of the greater rate of shrinkage the result is a textured cloth suitable for garments.

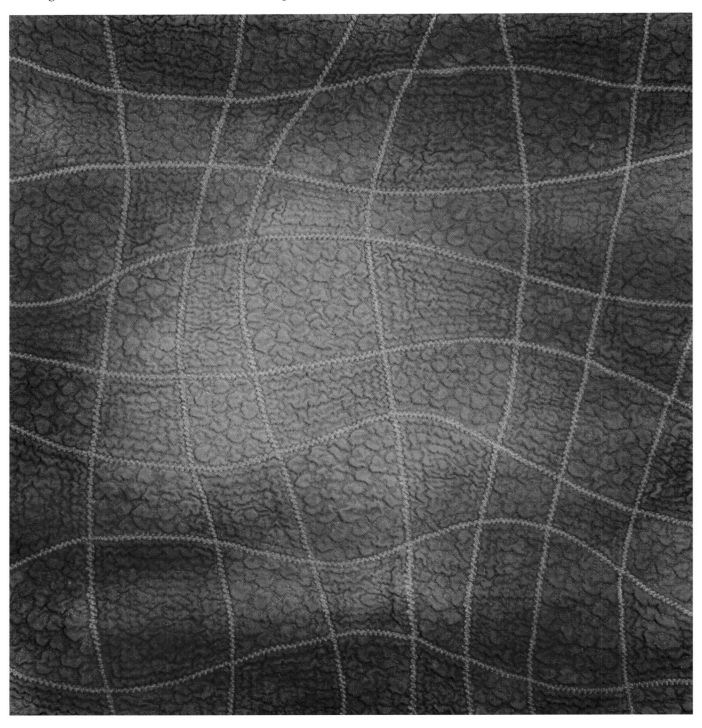

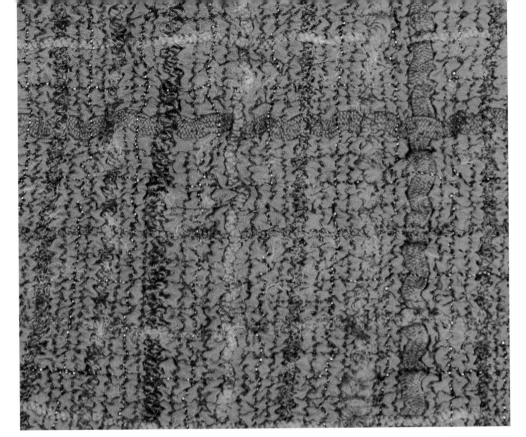

Opposite: **Applied Braids** (detail).

Above: **Grid Lock** (detail).

Right: **Glimpses** (detail).

Exercise 3
Using varying weights of fabric

SLAP AND STITCH

Gather a selection of small pieces of natural-fibre fabrics in different weights. It is important to include both heavier fabrics, such as canvas, furnishing weights and denim, and lighter ones such as silks or gauze. If you have a bag of samples from suppliers these are ideal.

1. Cut a piece of wool viscose felt or Arctic wool gauze up to twice the required finished size of the piece you want to make.
2. Lay pieces of fabric on this one at a time and free-machine them in place. Continue stitching pieces in place, leaving the raw edges of fabric to overlap each other slightly.
3. Pieces can vary in shape and size.
4. Add further stitching if desired, using free-machining.

Consciously lay fabrics of contrasting weight next to one another. By mixing heavyweight fabrics with lightweight and mediumweight fabrics the rate of shrinkage will be uneven resulting in undulation and distortion.

    Heart and Soul (opposite) was worked onto Arctic wool gauze and reduced by nearly 50 per cent when shrunk. *Turquish Delight* (below) was made using various weights of fabric in log cabin blocks on wool viscose felt.

Below: **Turquish Delight** (detail).

Opposite: **Heart and Soul** (detail). In this piece, samples of fabrics of various weights were 'slapped and stitched' onto Arctic wool gauze. It shrank by nearly 50 per cent.

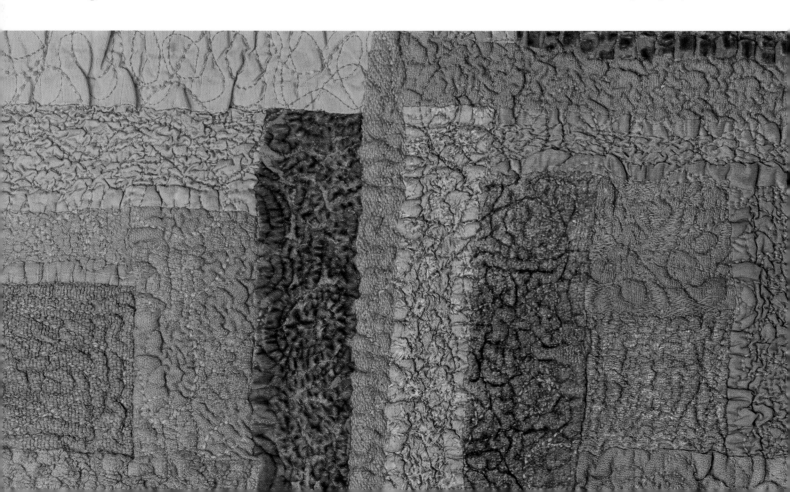

Exercise 4
Using strimmer nylon

Strimmer nylon creates fantastic twists and undulations on the surface as it does not shrink and forces the work to distort. The work needs to be stretched and secured to a mounting board to be displayed as it ends up as a mangled ball after processing.

REQUIREMENTS
- A piece of plain, white natural-fibre fabric – although the nylon can be used with pieced work
- Wool viscose felt or Arctic wool gauze
- Water-soluble thread
- Strimmer nylon – 1.3 to 1.5mm (0.05in to 0.06in) gauge works well. Milliners' wire can also be used but is not as flexible.

1. Lay the strimmer nylon as required on the **underside** of the top layer of fabric. Set the width of the zigzag stitch wide enough to bridge the nylon. Avoid stitching through it.
2. Use water-soluble thread to stitch the nylon in place. It will disappear with washing, leaving the surface of the fabric over the nylon smooth and free of stitch.
3. Layer the fabric on the wool viscose felt, placing the strimmer nylon on the underside between the top layer and the batting. Secure with safety pins.
4. Replace the water-soluble thread with cotton thread. With the feed dogs up and a zip foot attached, stitch along the sides of the nylon without stitching through it. Careful use of a twin needle with a pin-tuck foot fitted is an efficient way of stitching the nylon in place. Secure the ends of the nylon to stop the nylon from 'escaping' in the shrinking process. Stitching a bank of stitches at the ends or doubling it back on itself works.
5. Stitch the areas between the nylon to create texture as preferred.
6. Wash and dye in a tray following the low-immersion dyeing instructions on page 38.
7. Embellish as required and mount onto a board.

Above: **Singing the Blues**
28 x 68cm (10½ x 27in)
I used both strimmer nylon and applied viscose cord in this piece.

Opposite: **Undercurrents**
40 x 60cm (16 x 24in)
The surface of this piece was embellished with Markal (Shiva) Paintstiks.

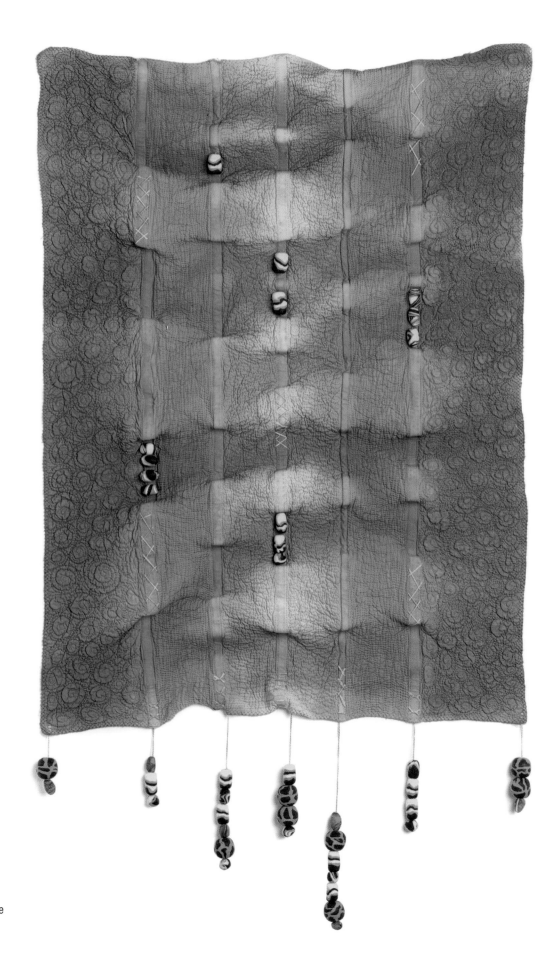

Exercise 5

Introducing package strapping or boning

REQUIREMENTS
- Top layer of plain, white, natural-fibre fabric
- Wool viscose felt
- Water-soluble thread
- Lengths of package strapping or Rigilene – could be various widths
- Embellishment to suit

Package strapping in various widths, weights and colours is a free material for shrinkage manipulation. It is forced to undulate when the work is shrunk, giving superb results. Bent tape can be ironed flat before using; use medium heat and protect the iron with parchment paper. Rigilene and twill-covered boning, available from specialist haberdashers, is a good alternative. Snip the corners of the tape to prevent it cutting through the top fabric. Two methods of incorporating strapping are explained here.

Applying strapping to the underside of the top layer

1. Make a rough sketch of how you plan to stitch the design.
2. Transfer this plan onto the fabric for guidance, or stitch freely, referring to the illustration.
3. Lay the strapping onto the **underside** of the top layer of fabric. Set a zigzag stitch wide enough to bridge the strapping if possible, otherwise stitch through it.
4. Working from the underside, with water-soluble thread in the machine, stitch the strapping in place. The water-soluble thread holds the strap in place temporarily and will wash away, leaving the surface over the strapping stitch free.
5. Layer the fabric on the wool viscose felt, placing the strapping on the underside between the top layer and the batting. Secure with safety pins.
6. Replace the water-soluble thread with cotton thread. With feed dogs up and a zip foot fitted, stitch along the outside edges of the strapping without stitching through it. Secure the strap ends by stitching through them to prevent them from escaping after washing.
7. Stitch the other areas around the strapping as preferred to create texture.
8. Wash and dye following the low-immersion dyeing instructions on page 38.
9. Embellish and mount on board.

Left: **The Green Piece**
42 x 60cm (16¾ x 24in)
This piece is embellished with beads
made from polymer clay.

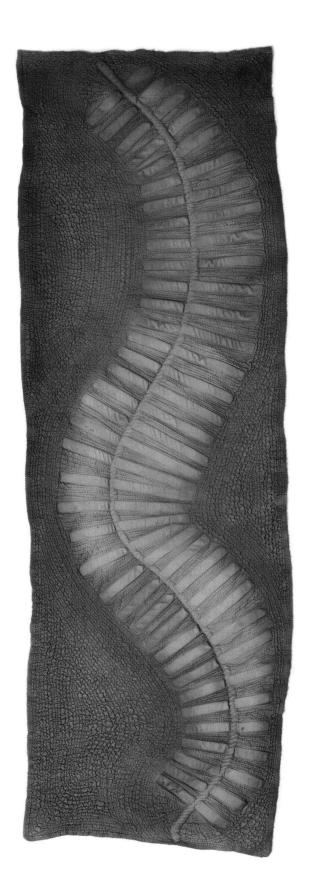

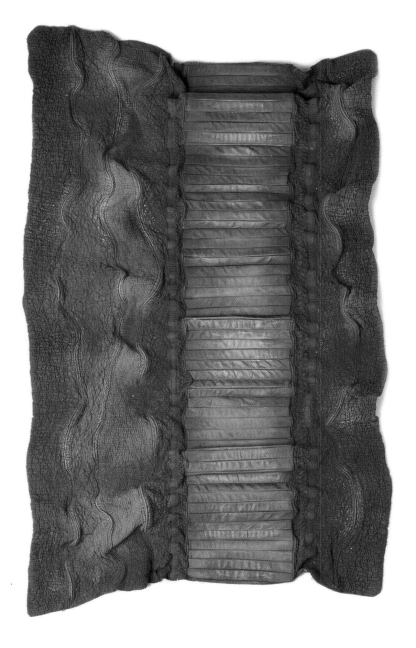

Left: **Ridgeback**
33 x 106cm (13 x 42in). Thick cord was combined with short strips of package tape.

Below: **Rocky Road**
48 x 95cm (19 x 38in).

Right: **Turbulence** 17 x 47cm (6¾ x 18¾in). A combination of strimmer nylon and package strapping was used to create undulations on the surface of this piece.

Below right: **Blue Divide** 22 x 30cm (8¾ x 12in). Extra layers of batting were used together with package tape and nylon to distort this surface.

Below: **Pathways** 28 x 41.5cm (11 x 16½in)

Securing package strapping in pockets

EXTRA REQUIREMENT
- Lightweight non-woven interfacing
- Water-soluble thread
- Strimmer nylon

1. Cut a strip of interfacing the size of the area in which you want to include the strapping.
2. Mark this with lines marginally wider than the strapping to be used.
3. Attach the interfacing to the **underside** of the top fabric by stitching down the length on one side.
4. Next, following the marked lines, stitch channels to slip the straps into, leaving one end open. Use water-soluble thread if you do not want double lines of stitching on the finished piece.
5. Cut pieces of strapping a little shorter than the channels and slip them into the sleeves.
6. Stitch along the open ends of the channels to hold the straps in place. See diagram below.
7. Add any further strapping and/or strimmer nylon to the underside of the channels using water-soluble thread.
8. Layer the fabric onto wool viscose felt, placing the strapping on the underside between the top layer and the batting. Secure with safety pins.
9. Replace the water-soluble thread with cotton thread. Free-machine stitch along the channels and the sides again to secure them to the felt.
10. Stitch the other areas around the strapping as preferred to create texture.
11. Wash and dye following the low-immersion dyeing instructions on page 38.
12. Embellish and mount on board.

This method was used in *Rocky Road* (page 94) to trap shorter strips of strapping that were laid side by side down the length of the work. Strimmer nylon and lengths of strapping were added down the length of the piece. In *Pathways* (page 95) zips were added alongside the strapping. See also *Spine Tingling* on page 16.

To make bulges as in *Un-Zipped* (page 79), *Test Case 1* (opposite) and *Test Case 2* (page 117):

1. Draw a circle on a piece of interfacing or Arctic wool gauze.
2. First secure a button in the centre of the circle and stitch around it with water-soluble thread.
3. Stitch channels for pieces of strapping to go into. See diagram opposite.
4. Slide the strapping in place, trimming the corners to avoid damage to the fabric.
5. When all the strapping bits are in place, stitch around the outside of the circle to hold them in place.
6. After layering the work onto wool viscose felt, stitch around the circle, button and strapping again, this time using cotton thread.
7. Quilt loosely between the strapping.
8. Wash, shrink and dye.

Opposite: **Test Case 1** (detail).

Below: Securing package strapping in pockets.

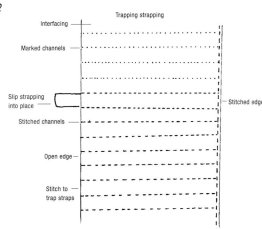

Below: Securing package strapping in circles.

Interlining or wool gauze

Stitch channels to
trap strapping

Secure button
and stitch
around it

When all straps are
trapped, stitch
around the circle

Fig 1 Underside of top layer

Quilt between straps

Restitch around tape
and circle onto batting

Fig 2 Top/right side

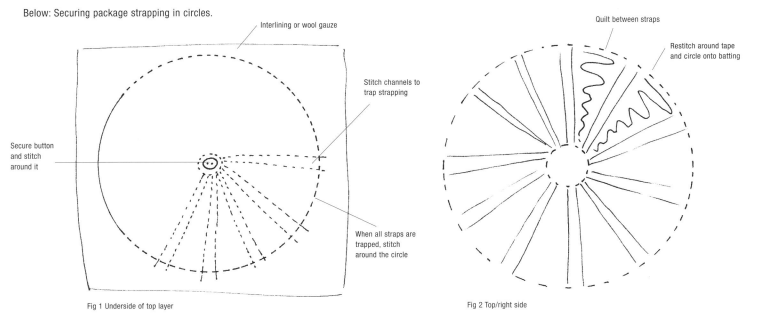

Exercise 6
Including buttons for texture and distortion

Buttons inserted beneath the top layer of fabric add interest and detail to the work. They can be used as a feature, as in *Pushing Buttons* (opposite), or as detail, as in *Spine Tingling* (page 16), *Octopus's Garden* (page 124), *Test Case 1* (page 97), *Test Case 2* (page 117) and *Under-Belly* (page 117).

There is not always enough clearance underneath the darning/quilting foot to accommodate the button. Some machines will stitch without a pressure foot – keeping the surface taut with your hands helps. Otherwise the work needs to be stabilized in a hoop. Mind your fingers! The quilting foot (no. 29) for early Bernina machines has a greater clearance and is invaluable for this technique. You may have to resort to hand stitching.

REQUIREMENTS
- Top layer of plain, white natural-fibre fabric
- Water-soluble thread
- Wool viscose felt
- Lightweight non-woven interfacing
- Collection of buttons in various sizes

1. Make a rough sketch of how you plan to place the buttons. Consider combining them with other materials such as strimmer nylon or strapping.
2. The buttons can be stitched onto the underside of the top layer by machine, using water-soluble thread. Use an open-toed or darning foot if you do not have a dedicated button foot. Lower the feed dogs and set the stitch width to accommodate the holes in the button. Three stitches are sufficient to keep the button in place temporarily.
3. Alternatively, for a more structured design – a grid or rows of buttons – draw a plan on interfacing. Place this on the **underside** of the top layer of fabric and stitch rows to slip the buttons into. Use water-soluble thread in the machine if preferred.
4. For a grid of buttons, first stitch columns the width of the buttons. Stitch one end of the columns closed. Slide a button down each column and then use a zip foot to stitch across the pockets close to the row of buttons in order to hold the row in place. Continue adding rows until the columns are full.
5. When all the buttons are in place, layer the fabric on the wool viscose felt, placing the pockets on the underside between the top layer and the batting. Secure with safety pins.
6. Replace the water-soluble thread with cotton thread. Carefully free-machine stitch around the edges of the buttons.
7. Stitch the other areas as required to create texture.
8. Wash and dye following the low-immersion dyeing instructions on page 38.

In *Under-Belly* (page 117) and *Spine Tingling* (page 16), buttons were combined with strapping for interesting effects.

Opposite, top: **Pushing Buttons** (detail).

Opposite, bottom: how to include buttons.

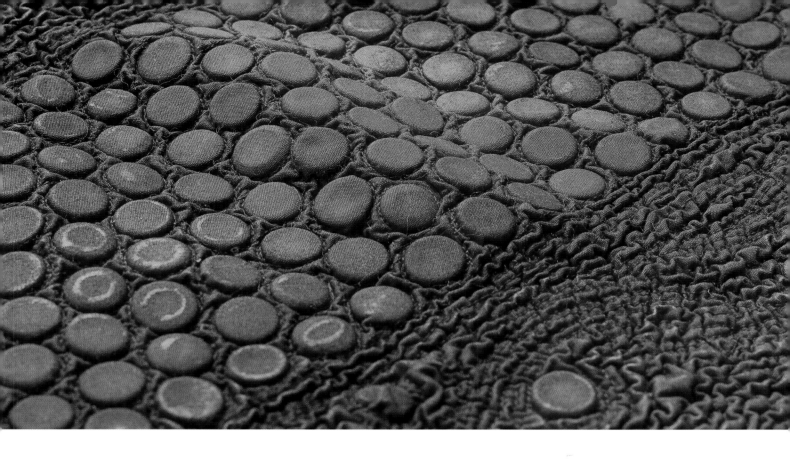

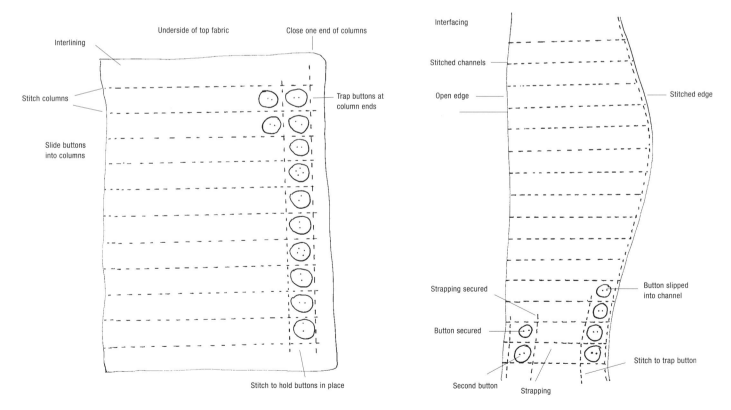

Fig 1 Trapping buttons

Fig 2 Trapping buttons and strapping

Fig 1 labels:
Interlining
Underside of top fabric
Close one end of columns
Stitch columns
Slide buttons into columns
Trap buttons at column ends
Stitch to hold buttons in place

Fig 2 labels:
Interfacing
Stitched channels
Open edge
Stitched edge
Strapping secured
Button secured
Second button
Strapping
Button slipped into channel
Stitch to trap button

Exercise 7
Zips combined with mosaic fabric

REQUIREMENTS

For a piece of mosaic fabric 60cm x 60cm (24in x 24in) you will need:
- Four 10cm (4in) squares in nine different fabrics (36 squares)
- Four squares of fusible Vilene, 30cm x 30cm (12in x 12in)
- Cotton thread
- Rotary cutter and board
- Plain fabric 90cm x 60cm (36in x 24in) viscose satin, cotton sateen or similar
- Wool viscose felt
- Cotton metal zips – the longer the better. Opened, pulls removed and pull ends trimmed.

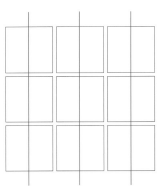

Fig 1

MOSAIC CONSTRUCTION

The aim is **not** to get accurate seams and corners – irregular cutting and joining will give a lively, informal look.

1. Organize the squares into four groups of nine squares, one of each fabric.
2. Arrange each group of nine squares on the fusible/rough side of the fusible Vilene. Arrangements could be identical or varied. Fuse the squares onto the Vilene.
3. Stitch along the adjacent edges of the blocks with a zigzag or decorative stitch wide enough to catch both raw edges.
4. Rotary-cut through the centre of each row of blocks in the vertical direction (fig 1).
5. Rearrange these strips so that no two fabrics are alongside one another, swapping and rotating as necessary.
6. Butt the strips up to one another and join them together in the new arrangement using the same stitch as before.
7. Turn the piece around so that the oblongs are now lying horizontally. Cut through the centre of each row of half blocks.
8. Rearrange the cut strips so that the fabrics are mixed up. Join these strips together, ending up with a block of 6 x 6 5cm (2in) squares (fig 2).
9. Repeat the process of cutting through the centre of each row of blocks and rearranging the strips to create a block of 12 x 12 2.5cm (1in) squares.
10. Repeat this process with each of the sets of nine blocks and join them together with the same stitch. For a larger piece create further blocks in the same way – consider using other fabrics to add variety.

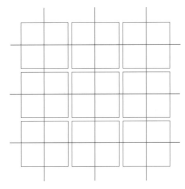

Fig 2

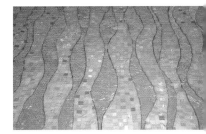

Fig 3 Quilting the spaces between the zips.

Fig 4 The piece after dyeing

QUILT ASSEMBLY

1. Cut the piece of mosaic fabric into five or seven strips – these could be straight-edged or curved.
2. Lay the plain fabric on the felt and pin.
3. Arrange the mosaic strips across this sandwich evenly, starting with the straight-edged side pieces and leaving gaps of the base fabric in between. Try mixing curved strips around for the most interesting arrangement. Pin the strips in place, removing any pins from under the mosaic-fabric strips.

Opposite: **Fire in my Soul**

125 x 145cm (50 x 58in)

(Photograph: Ole Hendriksen)

4. Stitch the strips down through all layers, slipping the tape edge of the zips between the strips and background as you go. Add zips as you go, end to end if they are not long enough to reach right across.
5. Quilt the spaces in between the zips (fig 3 on page 100).
6. Wash and dye in a tray following the low-immersion dyeing instructions on page 38.

ALTERNATIVE METHODS OF INCLUDING ZIPS
- Inserted into seams in the standard method.
- Stitched into tucks or pleats in the top fabric.
- Applied or couched – to do this, trim away the cloth close to the metal teeth and zigzag the metal braid onto the sandwich.

Heavily Disguised (opposite, and shown step by step below) was made for the Mary Fogg challenge, using fabrics donated by her to the Quilters' Guild of the British Isles. I assembled the fabrics using the mosaic method (1). Many of the fabrics had wool content and so I pre-dyed the assembled fabric with a purple acid dye (2). The assembled piece (3) was dyed with Procion dye flat on the patio. The coloured fabric turned out to be synthetic and didn't dye (4)!

1.
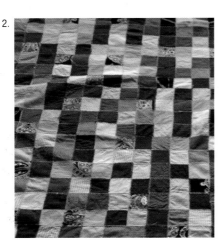

2.
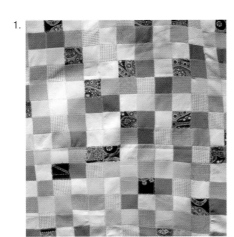

3.

Opposite: **Heavily Disguised** (detail).

Exercise 8

Inserting plastic shapes into layers

Placing shapes beneath the top layer can produce more specific effects.

SPECIFIC REQUIREMENTS
- Top layer of plain natural-fibre fabric
- Wool viscose felt
- Water-soluble thread (optional)
- Glue stick
- Lightweight non-woven interfacing
- Sheets of pelmet Vilene or firm plastic

1. Make a rough sketch of how you plan to place the plastic. If the shapes are to be placed in a design such as in *In a Spin* and *Sunflower* (opposite) draw the plan full-scale on interfacing, remembering to reverse the design. The interfacing will outline the design and also hold the plastic in place.
2. Trim the interfacing closer to the placement areas to allow easier access.
3. Pin the plan onto the **underside** of the top layer.
4. Cut out plastic shapes as required – number them to key them to their designated spot.
5. Slip the shapes into place between the fabric and interfacing, lining them up with the design. Hold them in place between the top layer and the interfacing with a dab of glue and stitch around them with free-machine stitching to hold them in place, using water-soluble thread if preferred.
6. For a more random placement of shapes, place each plastic shape on the wrong side of the top fabric and cover it with a piece of interfacing. Pin in place and free-machine around the plastic to trap it in place. If the shapes are regular in shape (squares or rectangles), a pocket of interfacing could be stitched first and then closed after the plastic has been inserted.
7. Pelmet Vilene or similar soft material can be stitched in place from the top. Mark the shape as required on the top layer. Lay a piece of the material to be added (big enough to cover the whole of the design) on the underside of the fabric behind the marked shape. Stitch around the shape from the front, turn the work over to the back and trim excess material away. Use water-soluble thread if you do not want these stitches to show.
8. When all the additions are in place, layer the fabric onto the felt, placing the pockets or applied pieces between the top layer and the batting. Secure with safety pins.
9. If you have used water-soluble thread, replace it with cotton thread. Carefully free-machine stitch around the edges of the shapes again.
10. Free-machine around the shapes again through all layers, and stitch other areas as required to create texture.
11. Wash and dye following the low-immersion dyeing instructions on page 38.

For *In a Spin*, Arctic wool gauze was used instead of the interfacing to trap the plastic. The spaces behind the plastic were stitched only between every other piece after the work was layered onto the felt, encouraging the plastic to 'zigzag'.

Opposite, top: **In a Spin**
74 x 33cm (29½ x 13in)

Opposite, bottom: **Sunflower**
(detail). Pelmet Vilene was used for the sunflower petals in this piece.

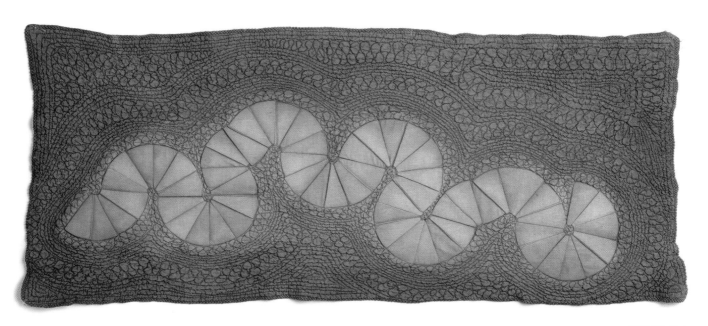

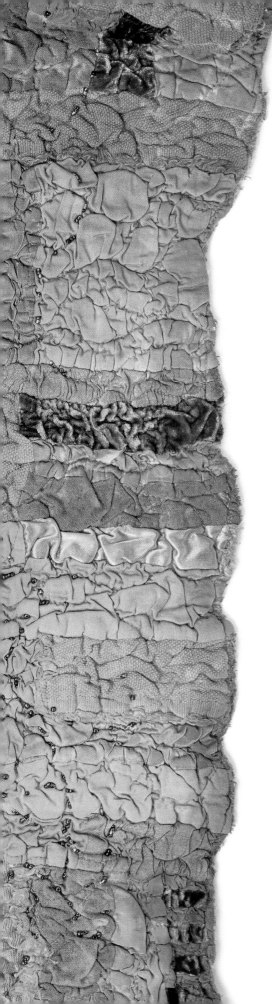

Shrinkage Gallery

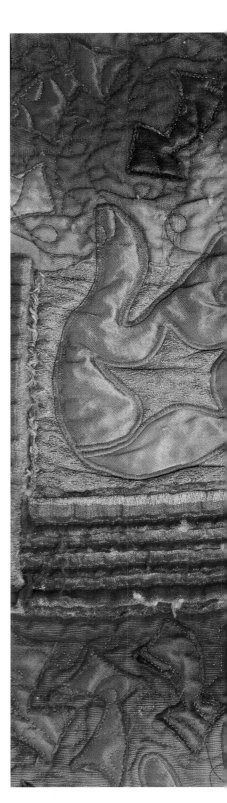

Right: **Mixed Metaphors** (detail).
Multiple layers of wool viscose felt and cotton batting
were alternated to achieve enhanced texture in this quilt.
Leslie Morgan.

Left: **How Can You Laugh...When You Know I'm Down?**
(detail).
This piece was first stitched onto a layer of wool viscose
felt, shrunk, and then re-layered onto another layer of felt
before being shrunk again. A range of gradation grey
fabric was used. The piece is about climbing out of a pit
of depression.

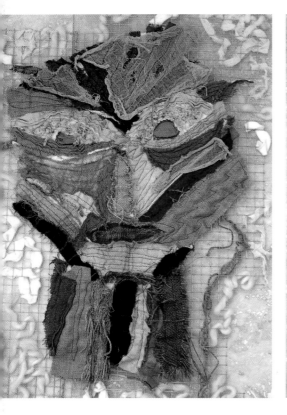

Above left: **Verdigris Centre**
23 x 28cm (9 x 11in)

Above right: **Brooch**
5 x 4cm (2 x 1¾in). Louise Grundy.
In these two pieces fabric was
sandwiched between two layers of felt.
The design was stitched and then the
top layer of felt was cut back to reveal
the fabric before shrinking and dyeing.

Left: **Face 1** 33 x 50cm (13 x 20in) and
Face 2 28 x 40cm (11 x 16in)
Shrinkage was used to coax expression
and character out of these faces. Sue
Lewis. Photograph: Garry McNamara.

Opposite: **Volcanicity** (detail)
Thin plastic tubing was used to form
the crater-like shapes in this piece.

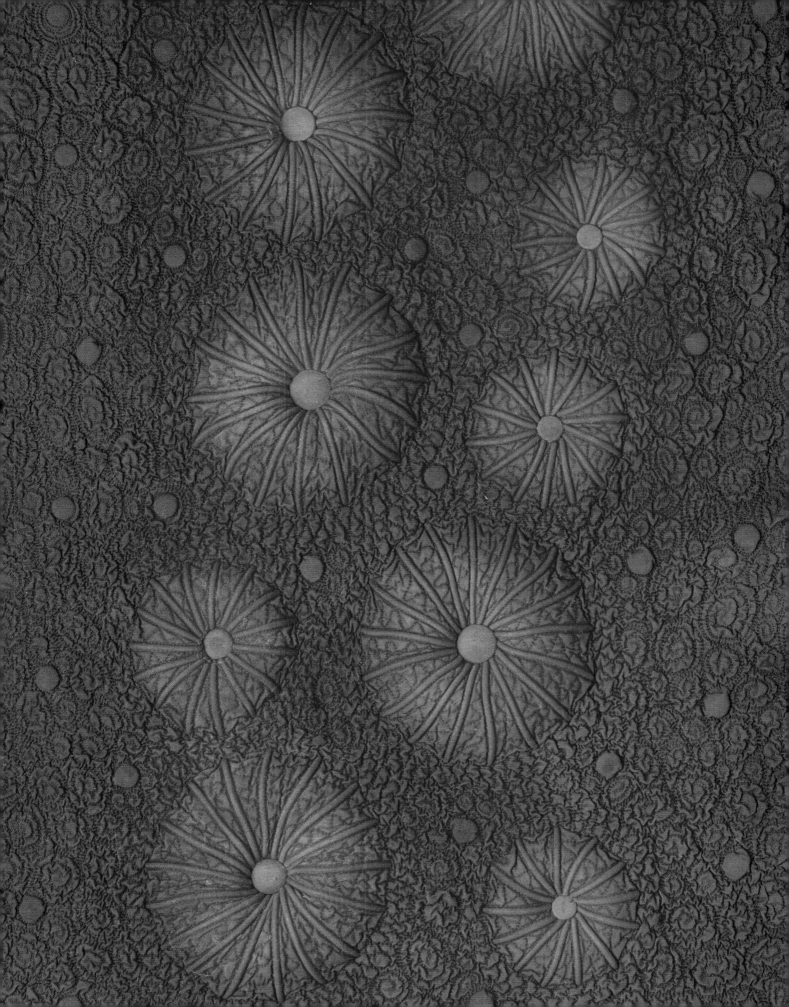

Left: **Book Cover**
The colouring of this book cover was inspired by a collection of beads. Sheila Acton.

Opposite and right: **Spring Garden** (opposite), **Summer Garden** (right, top) and **Autumn Garden** (right, bottom). All approx. 25 x 30cm (10 x 12in) Shrunken textile collages make great backgrounds for these refreshing embroideries. Gilly Pain. Photographer: Brian Lacey.

Opposite, top left:
Solstice Sunset
50 x 83cm (20 x 33in)
This is a sumptuous, richly
embellished piece, adorned with
fringes and stitch. It embraces
many of the techniques outlined
in this book.

Opposite, bottom left:
Zipping Along 1
24 x 38cm (9½ x 15in)
A combination of zips, nylon
and package tape were used in
this piece. Penny Tarbuck.

Opposite, right: **Acid Test**
32 x 65cm (12¾ x 26in)
'Slap and stitch' was combined
with foam padded areas and
pelmet Vilene in this piece.
Hand stitch and beads were
added after it was dyed.
Diana Shirley.

Left: **Field of Poppies 2**
42 x 76cm (16¾ x 30in)
Shrinkage was used to interpret
the subject in this piece.
Jackie Martin.

Left: **Fuchsia Blues**
47 x 67cm (18¾ x 26¾in)
This is another luscious piece that
embraces a range of different
materials to create varied effects.
Neredah McCarthy.

Right: **Rhapsody in Blue**
40 x 80cm (16 x 32in)
This piece is a perfect example of using
a combination of techniques to create
an intriguing playground of texture and
distortion for the eye (and fingers!)
to explore. Suzanne Fisher.

Left: **Hot Hot Hot**
48 x 78cm (19 x 31in).
Metallic thread was used to convey
a sense of heat in this piece.

Right: **Test Case 2** (detail).

Below centre: Inspirational sunrise
on Lady Elliot Island, Australia.

Below bottom: **Under-Belly**
82 x 37cm (32¾ x 14¾in).

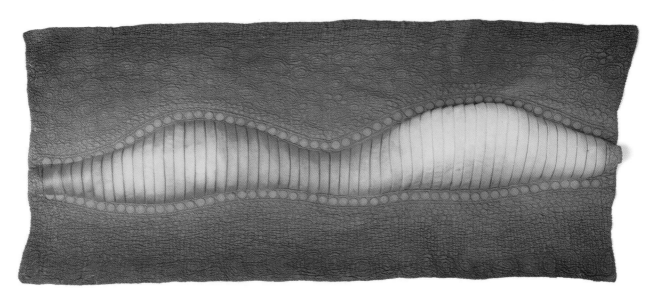

Left: **Tina's Bag**
Stitched and unstitched panels of white viscose velvet were combined and then dyed a deep burgundy to create this evening bag.
Tina Adcock.

Below: **Bag**
Zips were used to enhance the texture of the fabric used to make this bag. Jean Jackson.

Above: Reef

32 x 42cm (12¾ x 16¾in).

This piece was inspired by the skirt of a
clam seen on the Great Barrier Reef,
Australia (see page 11).

Finishing

Embellishment

When a piece is finished, consider whether it would be improved with embellishment. Don't embellish just because you can. Embellishment can be decorative or it can enhance the theme or message of the work. It should not clutter it with unnecessary adornment. It can draw attention and emphasize shapes or areas, or create interesting background areas (a grid of beads, for instance).

Many things can be used for embellishment. Found objects such as bottle tops, shells or driftwood) can be adapted to suit – they can be transformed with gold leaf or paint if they are a little gaudy. Holes can be made to stitch through.

Specific shapes and beads can be made from modelling clay, and items such as stones can be stuck to buttons with shanks or glued directly to the work surface. Consider anything that is interesting or would contribute to the work.

Ornament can be stitched onto or into the work, stuck on with suitable glue, or trapped under transparent fabric or a 'cage' of threads. It can be secure or hang free, offering movement and even sound. There are endless possibilities.

Above: **The Green Piece** (detail). Beads made of polymer clay were used to add embellishment to this piece (shown in full on page 92).

Below: Sheila Acton has used embellishment to good effect on her book cover. The colouring was inspired by a collection of beads.

Ornament

- **Beads**: strung they are useful for outlining a shape; individually they can offer interest to a background or highlight specific areas.
- **Buttons** with shanks are useful for applying other objects (such as dice or stones) to the work. Use epoxy glue. Other buttons can very effectively be used as eyes or for emphasis.
- **Sequins**: especially when combined with beads.
- **Plastic**: Friendly Plastic and Shrink Plastic can be used to make amulets to suit a theme.
- **Shisha Mirrors and Coins** can be secured with embroidery stitches, as can mosaic tiles, mirror tiles and pieces of glass. Small holes can be drilled into items such as coins to either stitch or suspend them to or from the surface.
- **Washers** and other **metal** bits and pieces such as zip pulls, nuts, split pins, chains, studs, metal eyes and bells are worth looking at. Specific shapes can be cut from aluminium or metal sheet.
- **Wire** – shapes can be formed from wire and attached to the surface with stitch.
- **Sundry items** – special plaques or ornaments can be made from paper and attached with stitch or adhesives.

The following are other ways of embellishing:

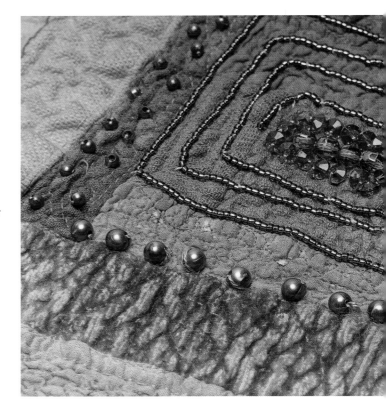

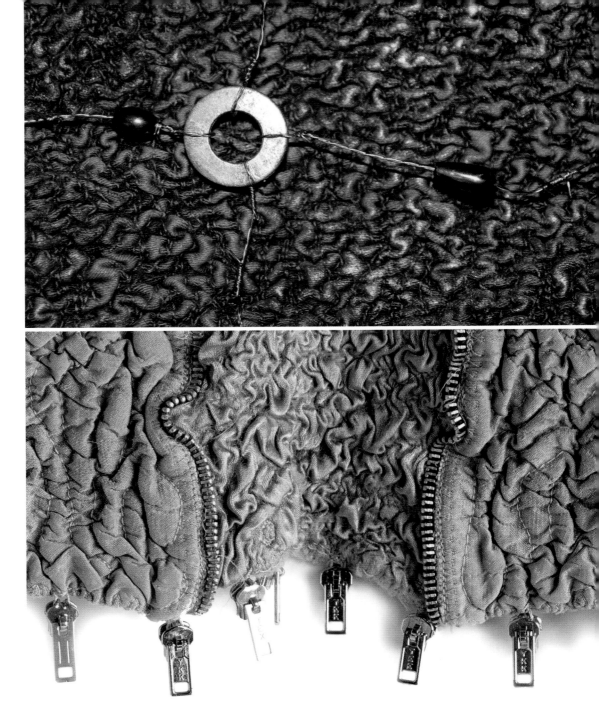

Right, top: **Mind The Gap** (detail).

Right, bottom: Zip pulls were used to emphasise the edge of this piece.

- **Paint** – products in the Texture Gel genre can be used to enhance the surface. Heavily stitched or raised areas can be enhanced by rubbing over them with Markal (Shiva) Paintstiks or metallic rubbing products. Acrylic paint can also be used to good effect.
- **Foil and gold/silver leaf** on the finished surface of the piece can be used to embellish the tips of raised surfaces.
- **Hand stitch** using chunky threads to add emphasis and/or decoration.
- **Embossing enamels.**
- **Tassels and fringes,** bobbles, wrapped cords and braids.

Presentation

The edges of most of the pieces worked in the exercises can be bound and finished in the usual way. However, I have found it very liberating not to bind a piece, leaving the edges raw, oversewing with a decorative stitch, or stitching cords and braids up to the edge. When leaving raw edges on Stitching to Dye work, ensure that the batting used is not polyester as this does not dye and stays white after the piece is dyed. Cotton batting without a stabilizer can create interesting edges. If there is a stabilizer on the batting it will stay white, so place it at the back of the quilt.

Most Stitching to Dye pieces can be hung on a conventional sleeve. Do not, however, attach a sleeve to shrinkage pieces until after all the dyeing has been done. At the time of dyeing, include a piece of fabric for a matching sleeve or the back of a cushion cover if necessary.

It is often not possible to hang the shrunken and distorted pieces on a sleeve. They need to be attached to something rigid such as a stretched canvas to support them. These come in various sizes, but it is possible to make them up if the right size is not available. They can be painted with acrylic paint to suit. The work can be either stitched onto the canvas, or glued with a glue gun.

Making and attaching a sleeve

1. Measure the width of the sleeve required – about 2cm (³⁄₄in) shorter at each end than the width of the piece so that the battens will not be visible.
2. Cut a strip of fabric this length – **plus** seam allowance for a folded hem on each end – and **twice** the depth of the required sleeve **plus** 4cm (½in) seam allowances.

   Note: all seams and turnings are on the outside of the sleeve, leaving the inside free of anything that will catch on the batten when it is passed through.

3. Stitch hems at each end, turned to the **outside** of the sleeve.
4. Fold the strip in half along the length, seams and hems to the **outside** (fig 1).
5. Stitch the raw edges together and press open.
6. Press the tube in half, placing the long seam at the centre of one side (fig 2).
7. Top-stitch about 0.5cm (¼in) from the folded edge along one of the pressed edges (fig 3).
8. With the seamed side at the back, shift the fabric so that the pressed line on the other edge is about 0.5cm (¼in) in from the edge. The excess material is on the unseamed edge, making a 'D' shape (fig 4).
9. Stitch along the pressed line – about 0.5cm (¼in) in from the folded edge.
10. Place the shorter seamed side of the sleeve flat against the quilt and stitch in place. Stitch the back edges at the sleeve ends to the quilt back so that the batten won't be pushed into the wrong opening.
11. The result is a sleeve with slack to accommodate the batten, allowing the quilt to be flat when the batten is in place. The back of the sleeve tube protects the quilt from the batten, preventing any damage to the quilt.

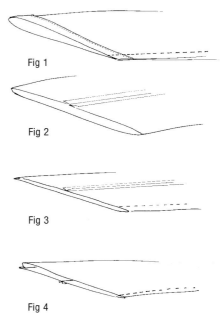

Fig 1

Fig 2

Fig 3

Fig 4

Above: Making a sleeve.

Troubleshooting

Inevitably, things will go wrong, especially in the dyeing department. First efforts are always a hit-and-miss affair; experience will improve matters. Sometimes there is nothing else to do but file the piece in the bin! There is no point in flogging a dead horse, but document the discoveries you have made and learn from the results so that you do not repeat the problem. Sometimes the colour is too pale, too vibrant, blotchy or just not to your liking. Don't give up too soon. Often pieces which are not successful as wall hangings can be turned into very successful bags, clutch purses or book covers with stitch and embellishment.

There are usually good reasons for the various problems and you can take steps to remedy most situations.

COLOURS TOO PALE

- Check that the fibre content of the fabric was 100 per cent natural.
- Did you forget to add soda ash?
- Was your dye strength too weak?
- Was the dye solution too cold or hot?
- Did you leave it to fix for long enough?

BLOTCHY, UNEVEN RESULTS OR SPOTS OF COLOUR

- Did you take time to blend the colours as you applied them?
- Did you use enough dye mixture? It needs to flood the work. Too little dye means the colours cannot blend into one another.
- Did you make sure that the dyes were well mixed, straining a couple of times to remove undissolved dye particles?
- Did you let the work dry out while it was colour fixing, causing the dye to oxidize and make dark streaks?

CONSIDER THE FOLLOWING REMEDIES:

- Over-dye to introduce other colours. Most pieces I make have been dyed from three to eight times!
- Remove as much colour as possible with bleach or a commercial colour stripper and then dye again.
- Add fabric paints or texture gels.
- Introduce Markal (Shiva) Paintstiks, rub on highlighting paints or gold or silver leaf.
- Embellish with hand stitch to disguise disappointing areas.
- Attach beads, gems, rhinestones or cabochons with adhesive.

Below: **Checkmate** (detail).

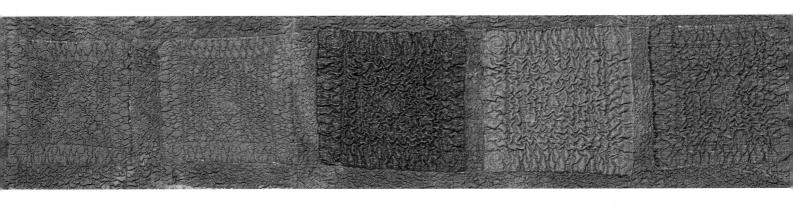

Conclusion

I have held your hand thus far. Now is the time to explore the endless possibilities. If you allow your imagination to run, ask many 'What ifs . . . ?' and search for answers, you **will** make discoveries. There are bound to be disappointments, and 'failures', but without these there will never be any successes. Work to please yourself, to achieve results that excite you and make you happy. There is nothing more pleasing!

If you don't try things out for yourself you will never know. Your results may not look like mine. You will probably interpret things differently, ask questions I have not asked and think of avenues to pursue that I haven't. This means that what you achieve can be individual and unique.

The ideas laid out in this book are by no means rules – they are a narrative of what happened when I answered the questions I asked. Perhaps deviation is the mother of invention! Go for it and enjoy the journey!

Below: **Octopus's Garden** (detail). A combination of buttons and nylon was used to create undulations on the surface of this piece.

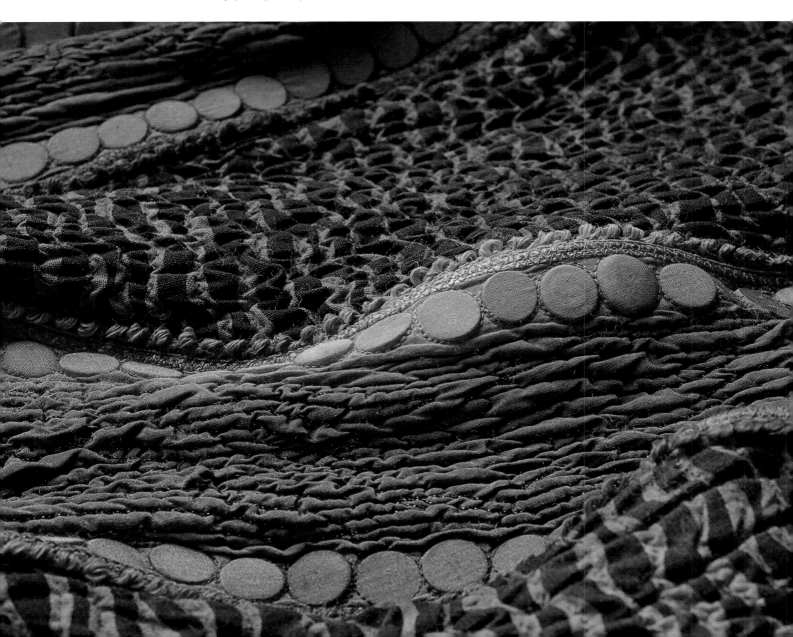

Appendix: Table of measurements

(Width × Height)		Before Washing		After Washing		Filling
		Metric cm	Imperial inches	Metric cm	Imperial inches	
Stitching to Dye						
Exercise 1	Finding Your Feet	92 × 92	36 × 36	84 × 84	33 × 33	Cotton
Exercise 2	Roaming in the Gloaming	77 × 112	30½ × 44	74 × 107	29 × 42	Cotton
Exercise 3	Black and Blue	77 × 110	30½ × 43	72 × 105	28 × 41½	Cotton
Exercise 4	Lime Zest	76 × 76	30 × 30	71 × 71	28 × 28	Cotton
Exercise 5	Strata	85 × 46	33 × 18	79 × 43	31 × 17	Cotton
Exercise 7	On the Shelf	60 × 33	23½ × 13	56 × 31	22 × 12½	Cotton
Shrinkage						
Exercise 1	Feeling the Heat	45 × 62	18 × 24	37 × 50	14½ × 20	WVF
Exercise 4	Octopus's Garden	97 × 92	38 × 36	79 × 54	31 × 21	WVF
Exercise 5A	The Green Piece	50 × 76	20 × 30	40 × 62	16 × 24½	WVF
Exercise 5B	Rocky Road	74 × 100	29 × 39	56 × 81	22 × 32	WVF
	Ridge Back	40 × 122	15½ × 48	33 × 106	13 × 41½	WVF
	Spine Tingling	38 × 127	15 × 50	33 × 110	13 × 43¼	WVF
	Test Case 1	39 × 70	14½ × 27½	26 × 50	10¼ × 19½	WVF
	Test Case 2	42 × 73	16 × 29	34 × 58	13¼ × 23	WVF
	Volcanicity	52 × 78	20½ × 30½	40 × 64	16 × 25	WVF
Exercise 6	Pushing Buttons	44 × 63	17½ × 25	36 × 48	14 × 19	WVF
	Under-Belly	92 × 48	36 × 19½	82 × 38	32 × 15	WVF
Exercise 8	In a Spin	90 × 43	35½ × 17	74 × 33	29 × 13	WVF
	Verdigris Centre	34 × 34	13¼ × 13¼	23 × 28	9 × 10½	WVF

Making book covers and clutch purses

BOOK COVERS: FINISHED SIZES
A6 − 25 × 17cm (9¾ × 6¾in) − sleeves two × 17 × 9cm (6¾ × 3½in)
A5 − 34 × 23 cm (13¼ × 9in) − sleeves two × 23 × 9cm (9 × 3½in)
A4 − 46 × 32cm (18 × 12½in) − sleeves two × 32 × 10cm (12½ × 4in)

Turn one edge of the sleeves. Lay these on the wrong side at each narrow end of the rectangles. Pin in place and stitch 0.6cm (¼in) in from the edge, all the way around, thus securing the sleeves. Finish edge with decorative or zigzag stitching and slip over book ends.

CLUTCH PURSES
Using a piece of work two and a half times the length of the purse you want to make, estimate five equal divisions along the length. Fold so that you have an envelope with the flap half the size of the purse. Finish the edges as above, attach clasps/buttons and cord for handle.

Further Reading

Construction

Cox, Patricia and Maggi McCormick Gordon. *The Ultimate Log Cabin Quilt Book*.
  Collins & Brown, 2004
Seward, Linda. *Patchwork, Quilting and Appliqué*. Mitchell Beazley, 1996

Dyeing

Dunnewold, Jane. *Complex Cloth*. Martingale & Company, 1996
Johnston, Ann. *Color by Accident*. Ann Johnston, 1998
Johnston, Ann. *Color by Design*. Ann Johnston, 2001
Kemshall, Linda and Laura Kemshall. *The Painted Quilt*. David & Charles, 2008
Laury, Jean Ray. *Imagery on Fabric*. C & T Publishing, 1992
Morgan, Leslie. *Tray Dyeing*. Committed to Cloth, 2007

Stitch

Noble, Maurine. *Machine Quilting with Decorative Threads*. That Patchwork Place, 1998
Tinkler, Nikki. *Quilting With a Difference*. Traplet Publications Ltd, 2002
Wolff, Colette. *The Art of Manipulating Fabric*. K P Books, 1996

Liberated/African-American quilt-making

Arnett, William. *The Quilts of Gee's Bend*. Tinwood Press, 2003
Mazloomi, Carolyn. *Spirits of the Cloth*. Crown Publications, 1999

Learning and inner development

Rose, Colin. *Master it Faster*. Spiro Press, 2001
Meier, Dave. *The Accelerated Learning Handbook*. McGraw-Hill Professional, 2000

Specialist Suppliers

United Kingdom

Barnyarns (Ripon) Ltd
Canal Wharf
Bondgate Green
Ripon
North Yorkshire
HG4 1AQ
www.barnyarns.co.uk
www.superiorthreads.co.uk
Fine threads, soluble thread and other supplies

Texere Yarns
College Mill
Barkerend Road
Bradford
BD1 4AU
Tel: +44 (0)1274 722191
www.texere.co.uk
Yarns in a wide range of fibres, blends, textures and colours

Kemtex Educational Supplies
Chorley Business & Technology Centre
Euxton Lane
Chorley
Lancashire PR7 6TE
Tel: +44 (0)1257 230220
www.kemtex.co.uk
Dyestuffs and chemicals

Colourcraft (C & A) Ltd
Unit 5
555 Carlisle Street East
Sheffield
S4 8DT
Tel: +44 (0)114 2421431
www.colourcraftltd.com
Dyes, paints, adhesives, craft materials

Whaleys (Bradford) Ltd
Harris Court
Great Horton
Bradford
West Yorkshire
BD7 4EQ
Tel: +44 (0)1274 576718
www.whaleys-bradford.ltd.uk
Wide range of natural-fibre fabric including wool viscose felt and Arctic wool gauze. They will ship internationally.

MacCulloch & Wallis
25–26 Dering Street
London
W1S 1AT
Tel: +44 (0)20 7629 0311
www.macculloch-wallis.co.uk
Boning, milliners' wire, bridal fabrics

The Silk Route
Cross Cottage
Cross Lane
Frimley Green
Surrey GU16 6LN
Tel: +44 (0)1252 835781
www.thesilkroute.co.uk
Wide range of silk fabric available in packs and cut pieces as well as by the length

Art Van Go
The Studios
1 Stevenage Road
Knebworth SG3 6AN
Tel: +44 (0)1438 814946
www.artvango.co.uk
Wide range of art supplies including dyes, paints, Markal (Shiva) Paintstiks and texture gels

Art Discount
Graphics House
Charnley Road
Blackpool, Lancashire
FY1 4PE
Tel: (+44) (0)1253 295743
www.artdiscount.co.uk
Stretched canvases and other art supplies

Naish Felts Ltd
Crow Lane
Wilton
Salisbury
Wiltshire SP2 0HD
Tel: +44 (0)1722 743 505
www.naishfelts.co.uk
Coloured wool and viscose felt in cut squares. Ships internationally

USA

Dharma Trading Co
Street address: 654 Irwin St. San Rafael, CA 94901
Store address: 1604 Fourth St. San Rafael, CA 94901
Tel: (800) 542-5227
and (415) 456-7657
www.dharmatrading.com
Just about everything – dyes, fabric, chemicals, advice

PRO Chemical & Dye
P.O. Box 14
Somerset, MA 02726
Tel: Orders only: (800) 228-9393
Customer service/technical calls: (508) 676-3838
www.prochemical.com
Dyes and chemicals

Index